SKETCHES FROM A LIBRARY WINDOW

SKETCHES FROM A LIBRARY WINDOW

BY

BASIL ANDERTON, M.A.

Essay Index Reprint Series

BOOKS FOR LIBRARIES PRESS, INC.
FREEPORT, NEW YORK

First Published 1923
Reprinted 1968

LIBRARY OF CONGRESS CATALOG CARD NUMBER:

68-16903

IOANNI WIGHT DUFF

DOCTORI LITTERARVM VTRIVSQVE IVRIS DOCTORI

PER TRIGINTA FERE ANNOS AMICO SPECTATO

HAEC SCRIPTA

QVIBVS NONNVNQVAM CONSILIO SVO SVBVENIT

D. D. D.

NEGOTIUM ETIAM IN ILLO OTIO REPERIO, ET INVENIT
IBI ANIMUS, QUOD SINE ACTIONE ULLA AGAT, SINE
LABORE ULLO ELABORET. . . . MENTI PARATI ILLI
[HORTI], NON CORPORI: AD EAM RECREANDAM, NON
AD HOC LAXANDUM: ET AD SALUBREM QUEMDAM
SECESSUM A CURIS ATQUE TURBIS.

LIPSIUS DE CONSTANTIA, II. 3.

A Stoic in His Garden[1]

INTRODUCTION

LIPSIUS' dialogue, *De Constantia*, was published about 1584[2] at Leyden. Belgium had long been in the turmoil of civil war. In 1572 Lipsius' own property had been pillaged whilst he was travelling. He had been to Liége to see his friend Charles Lange (or Langius), Canon of Saint Lambert,[3] and had afterwards gone on to Germany, Bohemia, and Saxony. After holding for a year or so a professorship at Jena, he returned to his home at Overyssche in 1575, by which time the civil war had subsided. But the troubles broke out again, and he had to fly to Louvain. Then in 1578, when the Spaniards entered Louvain, he went to Antwerp, and thence in 1579 to Leyden, where he had secured the chair of History.

His book, *On Constancy*, written, as he says, for his own edification, is an attempt to define the right attitude of a thoughtful man towards public evils such as Belgium endured. Lipsius wrote as a Stoic. Travel, he says, does not avail to cure the weariness and despondency which such evils induce. It is the mind itself which must be changed and made constant; and true constancy is founded on the judgments of right reason as distinguished from those of fickle opinion. The things which chiefly make assault upon our constancy are external good and evil things, both public and private. Of these, probably public evils (or reputed evils) are the most trying—such things, namely, as wars, pestilences, and tyrannies. Yet with regard to these public evils we should remember three things: (1) That we are prone, when apparently lamenting national sufferings, to be

---

[1] Reprinted from *The Library* by the kind permission of the Editor.
[2] Nisard, in *Le Triumvirat Littéraire* (pp. 60–2), gives 1583.
[3] Zanta, *La Renaissance du Stoicisme* (1914), p. 154.

really deploring our personal risks or mischances which are therein involved; (2) That an excessive (and erroneous) love of our country may lead us to bewail them overmuch. What, after all, is our own country? The space of a few fields? or the region bounded by certain mountain ranges? or is it, as Socrates held, the whole world? (3) That commiseration for those tossed on the waves of calamities may even be a vice. The sort of effeminate pity which faints at the sight of another's misfortunes is useless and mischievous; on the other hand, that inclination of the mind which prompts us to lighten helpfully the poverty or anguish of another is justifiable and right.

Coming then to the nature and origin of public evils, four main propositions, which form the backbone of the book, are advanced and argued concerning them: (a) That they are sent among us by the Providence of God, who is interested in and presides over all human affairs. (b) That they are necessary, and derived from Fate, in accordance with the law of mutation and death which obtains both throughout the physical world and throughout the affairs, the cities, and the kingdoms of man. (c) That they are advantageous to us in various ways, e.g. by training us to overcome difficulties; by admonishing us to keep to the right path, and not, in overweening confidence, to forsake it; and by chastising those who do wrong. (d) That they are neither intolerable nor novel: it is less the calamities themselves that we fear than the circumstances with which our imagination tricks them out; we always exaggerate, too, the afflictions of our own age in comparison with those of previous ages—wherein we are wrong, as is shown by an enumeration of the hosts of victims who suffered in certain old wars, famines, pestilences, and oppressions.

Of these four main propositions the second, third, and fourth are developed with some fullness. In the second, drawn from Necessity, and the perpetual "circle of beginning and ending," various definitions of Fate are given and expounded, as is to be expected in a book written on Stoic or Neo-Stoic lines. One point which is here brought out is this: To say that the evils are "fated" does not justify us in sitting with hands folded. It may also be "fated"—we do not know—that our personal efforts shall be the turning-point in their redress. The point is interesting in regard to the fatalistic attitude of certain Stoics. The third proposition deals with the methods of divine justice, with its sanction of these calamities, and with the apparent inequality of punishments. The fourth includes certain statistics—viz. of the slaughter of the Jews (a million and a quarter), and of the vast number of men and cities destroyed in Greek and Roman wars; to say nothing of the men, women, and children carried into captivity, or of the incredible mortality through plagues, starvation, organised murders by consuls or kings, etc. Compared with these appalling losses, Belgium's sufferings, Lipsius thought, were slight.

Such evils, then, are common to all nations. If we recognise clearly that they have formed part of human experience in all ages, we shall cease to be unduly perturbed by them.

The *De Constantia* is divided into two books; and the garden episode here translated makes an interlude at the beginning of the second part. The interlocutors are Lipsius himself and Langius of Liége, with whom Lipsius represents himself as having held this discussion when he visited him some years before in a flight from Belgium. Langius is the principal speaker, Lipsius the one to be convinced.

Editions of the text which are accurate and pleasant to read are hard to discover. The work would bear reprinting in times like these[4]; or even one of the old translations might be reproduced.

TRANSLATION OF THE 'DE CONSTANTIA' II. 1-3.

I.

ON the following day Langius thought he would take me to his gardens. He had them in two groups, which he looked after with watchful care, one being on a hill just opposite the house, the other lying a little further off on

[4] 1916.

lower ground, beside the Meuse itself—that river which
"flows with smooth current through the pleasant town."[5]
So he caught me quite early in my room, and said, "Shall
we have a walk, Lipsius, or would you rather keep quiet
and sit still?" "I'll have the walk, Langius, by all means,"
said I, "if it's with you. But where shall we go?" "If
you'd like it, to my gardens," said Langius, "beside the
river. They are not a long way off, you'll get some exercise
en route, and you'll see the town; besides, the air is pleasant
and cooling in this heat." "Good," said I; "and indeed,
with you to guide me, no way would be wearisome—unless
it were to the ends of Asia." Thereupon we called for our
cloaks and put them on; we set off, and we arrived. At the
entrance I looked from point to point with a roaming yet
observant glance; I marvelled at the rich elegance and
well-kept order of the place. "You dear old man," said I,
"how delightful this is; how brilliant! It's a heaven you
have here, Langius, not a garden! Why, the very stars in a
serene night burn no more brightly than these flowers of
yours that flash and gleam in their variety! The vaunted
gardens forsooth of Adonis and Alcinous? They were
trifles compared to these, and empty toys." As I spoke
I went nearer, and drew some of the flowers close to my
nostrils and my eyes. "Which should I pray for first," I
said, "to become all eyes like Argus, or all nose like Catullus?
Each of my senses alike here gets refreshment and delightful
stimulus. Avaunt, ye odours of Araby! Ye smell vilely,
methinks, beside a fragance so pure, so truly celestial."
Langius pressed my hand caressingly, though he smiled.
"Let me say, Lipsius," he replied, "that neither I, nor this
rustic Flora of mine, can accept such urbane and dexterous
praise." I answered, "But, Langius, it is true. You think
I am flattering? I say seriously, and am honestly persuaded,
that the Elysian Fields are not Elysian compared with this
pleasance of yours. For see, what radiancy is here on all
sides! what order! how fittingly things are all set out in their
little beds and banks! No floor of mosaic could be worked
more daintily! Then what abundance of flowers and
herbage! what rarity and novelty! In this little enclosure,

[5] Quod per amoenam urbem leni fluit agmine flumen. Ennius.

one would think, Nature has concentrated every excellence of the old world and of the new."

II.

"AND I tell you it's a fine thing and a praiseworthy, Langius, this enthusiasm of yours for gardens—an enthusiasm into which, if I am not mistaken, all the best and most simple-minded men get drawn by Nature herself. In proof of this, it would be hard to name any pleasure about which, from all time, notable men have been so eagerly of one mind. Look through the Sacred Writings: what do you find? You will see that with the birth of the world came the birth of gardens, which God himself assigned to the first man as his dwelling, and, so to speak, as the abode of a happy life. And in profane writings? See how proverbs and legends tell of the gardens of Adonis, Alcinous, Tantalus, the Hesperides. In true and authentic histories, too, you will find that plantations of trees were begun by the hand of King Cyrus; flowers pendent in the air, by that of Semiramis; and, by that of Masinissa, a new and notable cultivation, that set Africa wondering. Then, too, among ancient Greeks and Romans how many famous persons I could recall who, laying aside other cares, gave themselves up to this care only. Among Greeks, you have, in a word, most of the philosophers and wise men; they left the city and the distracted agora and shut themselves within the walks and the hedges of gardens. Among Romans, I see King Tarquinius, far back in antique Rome, gently walking in his gardens, cutting off the heads of the poppies; Cato, the grave Censor, I recognise, devoted to garden affairs, and writing seriously about them; Lucullus, too, after his victories in Asia, I see taking his ease in them; Sulla, when he had given up the Dictatorship, therein quietly passing into old age; and the Emperor Diocletian valuing his cabbage and lettuce at Salona above all his purple and his sceptres. Nor has the crowd differed from the judgment of its betters; for I know that, among it, all men whose minds are simple, and free from evil ambition, have given themselves up to this art.

"Assuredly there is some secret and congenital force in us (though its origin I cannot readily explain), which draws us to this guileless and simple pleasure—draws, not only us who are disposed to yield, but even those grave and austere men who resist its pull and think scorn of it. And, as none may behold the firmament and its eternal fires without a hidden dread and awe, so none can see the divine wealth of the earth, and the fair order of this ordered world around us, without a silent thrill and sensation of delight. Question your heart and mind: they will say that such a sight captivates them, nay, feeds them. Question your eyes and senses: they will confess that in no place could they so willingly abide as among these garden beds and flowery banks. Stand, pray, about these swelling ranks of flowers; see how that one is bourgeoning from its cup, this from its sheath, yonder one from the bud; look at this one dying so suddenly, that other just coming to the birth; and observe lastly, in one species and another, the habit, the form, the features, so like in a thousand ways, and so diverse.

"What mind so rigid as not to unbend, amidst all this, in gentle thoughtfulness, and become softened? Come and give heed, eyes of mine! Fix yourselves a while on these radiancies and tints; look into this purple of nature's own, this blood colour, this ivory, this snow, this flame, this gold! and all those other hues such as an artist's brush may rightly emulate—emulate indeed, yet never equal. Lastly, what an exhalation of perfume is here! what a breathing and penetration! Surely some heavenly air is poured upon us from on high. It can be no empty feigning of our poet-folk when they say that most flowers are born of the essence and life-blood of the immortal Gods. Hail, thou true fount of joy and welling pleasure! Hail, thou abode of all Loves and Graces! Mine be it to possess my life in peace amid your shades! Mine, to be withdrawn far from civic tumults and to roam to and fro among these herbs and flowers—flowers of the known world and of the unknown—with glad, unsated eyes; and as this one droops down, and that one arises, to touch them and watch them; and in a haphazard waywardness to be here beguiled of all cares and labours."

III.

I SAID all this with some heat, and with eager voice and face. Langius' aspect was quiet as he said to me, "You are in love, Lipsius, you are certainly in love, with this flower-decked, purple-clad nymph; but I fear you love her intemperately. You praise gardens; yet in such a way as to show you admire their many empty or outward delights, whilst you neglect those that are true and legitimate. You gloat, I mean, over the colours, you rest on the banks, you search after flowers from the known and the unknown world. Pray, what is it you really think them? I would fain be sure that you too are not of that sect which has just arisen—a sect of busybodies and idlers—men who turn a very good and simple thing into an instrument of the two vices of Vanity and Laziness. That is the purpose with which they keep gardens. They get together vaingloriously some little herbs and exotic flowers, and having got them they coddle them and guard them more nervously than any mother her son. These are the men whose letters go hurrying about into Thrace, Greece, and India; and all for the sake of some tiny seed or trifling bulb. To these men the death of some new flower is more grievous than that of an old friend. We may laugh at that old Roman, Hortensius, who went into deep mourning for one of his fish; these do the like for their plant. Again, if one of these courtiers of Flora's has acquired some little novelty or rarity, how he displays it! how the other competitors rival and envy him! but some go home more gloomy than Sulla or Marcellus of old, when, as candidates for the Praetorship, they were beaten. What can we call it, but a kind of laughable madness, not unlike that of children who turn white and furious over their dolls and puppets? Then you must realise the industry of these same men in their gardens! They sit, they walk about, they yawn, they sleep —and naught else! so that, in fact, this is no retreat or leisure that they keep, but a burial-place of sloth. The ignorant crew! I would shut them out—and with justice— from the sacred rites of the true and secret garden; for I know it was designed for temperate pleasure, not for vanity;

for peace, not for torpor. Am I so light-minded that the
mere getting or losing of some paltry, little-known plant
shall make me exult or despair? Nay, I judge things at
their proper value. I strip off the meretricious show of
novelty; I know that they are plants, know that they are
flowers—that is, things shortlived and fugitive, about which
the great poet[6] says most rightly, 'Zephyr's breeze brings
some to the birth, others to maturity.' It is not, then,
that I despise this pleasure, or this beauty. You see the
evidence! But I differ from the soft school of Hortensius
in this, that I am untroubled in acquiring such things, untroubled in possessing them, untroubled in losing them.
Nor am I myself so withered, nay, so dead, as to hide away
and bury myself, as it were, in these garden shades. I find
occupation even in this leisure, and my mind here discovers
things which, making no ado, it can do quietly, which it can
elaborate without laboriousness. 'I am never less solitary,'
as has been said, 'than when alone; never less leisurely
that when at leisure.' It is an excellent saying; and I
would dare affirm that it originated in just such gardens as
these. Of a truth they are made for the mind, not the body;
for bringing renewal to the one, not slackness to the other;
in a word, for healthful retreat from care and 'the madding
crowd.' Are men wearisome to you? Here you will be in
your home. Has occupation exhausted you? Replenish-
ment lies here, where your mind may have the true food of
quietness, and may draw from a purer air the inspiration of
a new life. Wherefore, behold those Wise Men of old: it
was in gardens they dwelt. Behold those erudite and
learned souls of to-day: in gardens do they take their pleasure
wherein are mainly wrought and shaped those divine writings
at which we marvel, writings to which no sequence of years,
no old age, can bring surcease. To the green Lyceum how
many treatises on nature do we not owe? To the Academic
groves, how many on ethics? From garden walks, too, there
stream forth those rich rivers of wisdom from which we
drink, and which with their fruitful flood have washed the
whole earth. Truly, the mind rises and mounts nearer to
those high things when it is free and unshackled, when it
can behold its own sky, than when it is enclosed and kept

---

[6] Homer, *Od.* 7, 119.

fast in the imprisonment of houses or cities. Fashion here, then, O ye poets, some enduring song! Meditate and write here, ye men of letters! And do ye, O philosophers, argue here on tranquillity, on constancy, on life, and on death! See then, Lipsius, the true use and end of gardens: it is leisure, retirement, meditation, reading, writing; and all these, nevertheless, as if by way of relaxation and play. As painters, if their eyes have grown dull by long straining, restore them by looking in mirrors and on greenery; so we here restore our mind when it is weary or prone to wander. And why should I hide from you my own practice? Do you see that pergola, with its topiary art? That is my 'abode of the Muses,' that my gymnasium and wrestling-ground of wisdom. There I either fill my heart with abstruse and serious reading, or I implant, as it were, in it, the seeds of fruitful thoughts; and from these I store in my mind, like weapons in an armoury, precepts which anon are ready at call against the rough force and fickleness of Fortune. As soon as I set foot therein, I bid all common and ignoble cares remain aloof; and holding my head erect as may be, I watch beneath me the pursuits of the ignorant crowd and all the emptiness of human affairs. Nay, I seem to strip off from me the man, and to be caught aloft in the fiery chariots of Wisdom. Am I there, think you, tormented about the intrigues of the French or the Spaniards? about who keeps or loses the sceptre of Belgium? whether the tyrant of Asia threatens us by sea or land? or, in a word, ' what plan the king of the frozen north-land is brooding over?'[7] Not so. Fenced and shut in against outward things, I abide within myself. I am free from all cares save one: that is, to break in and tame my mind in submission to right reason and to God, and to subdue all other human affairs to my mind. So that whenever my last, fated day shall come, I may receive it with tranquil mien and without sorrow; and may go out from this life not as a man who is cast forth, but like a man set free. These, Lipsius, are my leisurely meditations in the gardens; these are the fruits which, so long as my mind keeps its health, I would not exchange for all the treasures of Persia or of the Indies."

[7] Quid sub Arcto | Rex gelidae meditetur orae [*vice* Quis sub Arcto | Rex gelidae metuatur orae. Horace, *Odes*, i. 26].

A Stoic of Louvain : Justus Lipsius[1]

THOUGH several books on Stoicism have been published of
late years, yet a work on the subject written by a bygone
scholar does not lose its attractiveness or its lasting qualities.
The old may well contain somewhat that is lacking in the
new. Such a treatise, for example, as Justus Lipsius issued
in 1604 may afford no small delight to one who spares time
to read it through. The book is now, it would seem,
tolerably rare—in England at all events. My own copy is
the 1644 edition. It is a volume small in size, but containing a good deal of matter, since there are in it over
750 closely-printed pages. It is a guide or handbook to
Stoic Philosophy and Physics, for illustrating Seneca and
other writers.[2] Lipsius had, in fact, a great admiration
for Seneca, both as a man and as a writer.

I propose, therefore, to give some account of Lipsius' life;
to give an outline of his manual on Stoicism; and, finally,
to touch on his attitude towards Seneca.

Materials for the life of Lipsius are not wanting. Of his
portraits, the one by Rubens, in "The Four Philosophers,"
was of course contemporary. Gudeman's *Imagines Philologorum*, too (published by Teubner in 1911), gives a likeness.
Lipsius' brief *Autobiography*, written in the form of a letter
to Woverius, a pupil, and edited separately by Bergmans
in 1889, likewise contains a portrait. Pökel's *Philologisches
Schriftsteller-Lexikon* gives a considerable and easily-
accessible list of publications by him, and some biographical
references. Miræus' *Vita Justi Lipsii*, written in 1606,
the year of Lipsius' death, is reprinted in the 1675 edition
of Lipsius' collected works (Wesel). There are also French

---

[1] A paper read to the Northumberland and Durham Classical Association,
in November, 1914.

[2] *Manuductio ad Stoicam philosophiam, etc., L. Annæo Senecæ aliisque
scriptoribus illustrandis.*

lives of him by Galesloot (1877) and Amiel[3] (1884), which
are mentioned in *Chambers's Biographical Dictionary*. Dr.
Léontine Zanta, in his *La Renaissance du Stoicisme au XVIe
siècle* (Paris, 1914), devotes ninety pages to Lipsius. Of
these, fifteen go to his life, fifteen to his *De Constantia*,
and the rest to his *Philosophia et Physiologia Stoica*. Zanta's
work is an important one on Neo-Stoicism—i.e. the fusion
between Stoicism and Christianity, which, as he holds,
Lipsius initiated. Lipsius' personality and learning receive
full recognition. *La Grande Encyclopédie*, in an article by
Hubert, devotes two full columns to his history, and mentions
several volumes that deal with him in detail. Nisard's
book, *Le Triumvirat Littéraire au XVIe siècle* (i.e. Lipsius,
Scaliger, and Isaac Casaubon), is full and valuable, and
shows acumen and learning. If it is not an over-sympathetic
study, it is yet in many respects appreciative.

Rubens' picture, known sometimes as "The Four Philosophers," sometimes as "Lipsius and his Pupils," is in the
Pitti Gallery, Florence. The other figures are Rubens
himself, his brother Philip (both of whom, according to
Dr. Johann Faber,[4] were pupils of Lipsius), and, according
to some, Hugo Grotius.[5] The following interesting description of the principal figure, Lipsius, is taken from Zanta
(p. 151): "His attitude is wonderfully appropriate to a learned
professor, such as Lipsius was all his life. His left hand
rests on a book, indicating some passage which he is explaining; whilst his right hand, half open and slightly raised,
seems ready for the rhythmic movement which so often
accompanies the orator's words. His look is a little fixed,
yet profound, and seems to be following his thought, and to
see nothing of the outward world. His angular face, which
a scholar's long and patient researches have marked with
premature lines, is the more conspicuous for the wide ruff

---

[3] *Un publiciste du XVIe siècle: Juste Lipse.*

[4] Faber was Rubens' friend and doctor. See the work mentioned in
the next note.

[5] Max Rooses, keeper of the Plantin-Moretus Museum, Antwerp,
comments on this picture in his *Rubens* (translated by H. Child: Duckworth
and Co., 1904). He thinks the fourth figure was Jan Woverius, mentioned
above. The picture was painted, he believes, in 1606, after the death of
Lipsius.

which frames it; a pointed beard accentuates the length of its contour." Similarly Rooses[6] says: "Justus Lipsius is here represented exactly as he is in the pictures and engravings of a later date; with a long, bony face, an unusually high forehead, a thin nose, hollow cheeks and sunken eyes, and a full beard; he is quite the scholar attenuated by study."

Lipsius was born at Overyssche, near Brussels, in 1547, and he died at Louvain in 1606. When six years old he went to a school at Brussels; when ten, to the college of Ath in Hainault. Then he was sent to the College of the Jesuits in Cologne. Here his teachers seem to have made a deep impression on him, and to have inspired a life-long affection, which in his last years influenced his final return to Roman Catholicism.[7] By the time he was sixteen he thought of joining the Jesuit Order. His father opposed this, however, and sent him to the University of Louvain, which, founded in 1423 (or 1425?), had reached in the sixteenth century the height of its fame, and counted 6,000 students on its roll. Let me say, in passing, that, although its numbers declined later, it always held the leading position in Belgium, and a year ago had still between 2,000 and 3,000 Catholic students on its books. At Louvain, then, Lipsius completed his education, working finally on law. On the death of his parents he gave himself up to the study of antiquity.

In 1569 he published his first work, *Variarum Lectionum libri IV.*—a collection of conjectures and commentaries on different authors, wherein he already exhibits his characteristic qualities, viz. his perfect knowledge of Latin and the lucidity of his critical method.[8] He went to Rome as Cardinal Perrenot de Granvelle's secretary, and there he stayed two years, giving his leisure to the inscriptions and ancient monuments, gaining access to the libraries (the Vatican amongst them), and gathering a harvest of notes for his future writings. He also came to know such Italian *savants* as Muretus, Manutius, Ursinus, Bencius, etc. He then returned to Louvain, where, according to some, "il mena, pendant le temps assez court qu'il passa dans sa patrie, une vie dissipée; suivant d'autres et suivant ce qu'il

---

[6] *Loc. cit.* vol. i. p. 97.   The picture itself is there reproduced.
[7] Žanta, *op. cit.*   [8] *Grande Encyclopédie.*

nous dit lui-même, il paya tout simplement son tribut à la danse et aux gaies réunions d'amis."[9]

In any case, being dissatisfied with this life, he set out for Germany, stopping at Liége to see his friend Langius, and at the University of Dôle, where he was well received   Here, in 1572, he had a nearly fatal fever, due partly, perhaps, to the excitement of a speech he had to make in honour of his friend Gisélin, and to a subsequent banquet.   Presently he travelled on to Vienna, where Cardinal de Granvelle's recommendation and his own reputation secured him a cordial welcome.   Maximilian II. tried to retain him by brilliant offers, but Lipsius valued his liberty, and refused. He continued his journey, on through Germany, to Bohemia, Prague, Thuringia, and Saxony.   Here he heard that a pitiless civil war had broken out in Belgium, and that his patrimony was endangered.   It was even pillaged.   He could do nothing, and was without resources; so he applied for, and obtained, in 1572, the Chair of Eloquence and History in the Protestant University of Jena.   Lipsius as a Catholic was in a delicate position.   His religious opinions seem to have become unsettled.   Did he go so far as con-version to Protestantism?   It is a matter of conjecture, definite evidence being wanting.[10]   Whatever happened, the persistent ill-feeling of his colleagues led, in March, 1574, to his resignation of the chair.   Going to Cologne, he met and married Anne Calstria, a widow older than himself. She belonged to a patrician family of Louvain, and was a strong Catholic.   Zanta thinks that she was one of the influences that brought about the final phase of pure Catholicism of his closing years.   They seem to have been tolerably happy together,[11] though she was of cross-grained disposition; they had no children.

Lipsius stayed nine months at Cologne, preparing philo-sophical and historical notes on Tacitus, of whom he pub-lished, at the end of the year, an excellent edition, elucidating many obscure passages.   Then, in 1575, he issued *Anti-quarum Lectionum lib. IV.* (comments and corrections on Plautus).   The civil war having subsided, he returned home

---

[9] Zanta, pp. 153–154.   [10] Zanta, p. 155.
[11] "Concorditer sane viximus," says Lipsius.

to Overyssche, hoping to live in studious retreat; but the troubles soon broke out again, and he had to fly once more. He went first to Louvain, where he resumed his legal studies, and in 1576 became *Jurisconsultus*. He also[12] collected and published the laws of the early Kings of Rome, and the law of the Twelve Tables. As Zanta says, "Quelle prodigieuse activité que celle de cet homme, qui, ballotté de tous côtés, à la suite des malheurs de sa pauvre patrie, sut néanmoins utiliser précieusement ses loisirs forcés pour la gloire des lettres." But the waves of war at last reached his new refuge. In 1578 the national army was destroyed at Jembloux, and the Spanish soldiery entered Louvain.[13] Lipsius fled to Antwerp; the room he occupied there for a short time in the Musée Plantin is still shown. Seeking once more for a livelihood, he again found it only among Protestants—viz. in the Calvinistic University of Leyden, where, in 1579, he was appointed Professor of History. Zanta has a line or two upon his religious position there, and the view is perhaps worth noting. He says: "Necessity had stifled all his religious scruples. Perhaps he thought, in self-justification, of the Stoic 'fatum,' against which it is mere folly to struggle; the Stoics alone were able to give him the excellent lessons of resignation of which he stood in need."[14]

The Leyden chair Lipsius held for twelve brilliant years. He himself, as he says in his *Autobiography*, thinks that here, in the full vigour of his years, he did his best work. Students came to hear him from distant lands; each year, too, "a new book bore witness to his potent activity and increased his reputation."[15] After various notes on Valerius Maximus,

[12] Zanta, and *Autobiography*.

[13] Concerning the recurrent woes of Belgium Dr. J. Wight Duff aptly observed that Lipsius' own words (in the dedication of his edition of Seneca to Paul V.) were as appropriate in 1914 as they had been more than three centuries ago : ecce iactamur, ac paene mergimur, fluctibus armorum simul et errorum.

[14] An interesting view of the whole question of Lipsius' apparent vacillation on religious matters was expressed by Canon A. H. Cruickshank, D.Litt., who thought that it was caused by a genuine intellectual difficulty in coming to a decision, and who quoted as a parallel the conduct of Cranmer in captivity.

[15] *Grande Encyclopédie*. Lipsius himself, in his *Autobiography*, mentions the titles of fourteen publications.

Seneca (*qua* tragedian), Velleius Paterculus, etc., he published in 1583 or 1584 his famous treatise *De Constantia*, which, as Zanta says, "seems to be a *résumé* of his philosophical reflections, and presents their author as a true Stoic." He was in exile, be it remembered, and his property was gone.

The book, which has made its appeal to very many readers, answered the preoccupations of the day. It had a great success, and was preferred to the more erudite of his works. By 1873 it had passed through more than eighty editions. Then came a new edition of his *Tacitus*; his *De recta pronunciatione latinæ linguæ dialogus* (1586), which reached fifteen or sixteen editions; and lastly his *Politicorum, sive civilis doctrinæ, libri sex* (1589), which by 1752 had passed through nearly eighty editions. In this work he seems, says Zanta, to exhibit "a return to the first form of his Catholicism, that born of his college years." It is a *résumé* of the precepts for government formulated by Latin writers. One of the chapters deals with the religious question, and to this chapter were due much hostile criticism and a noisy religious polemic. The Calvinists reproached him with being, in his advocacy of a single form of worship, an apologist for the Inquisition and for religious persecution. The Catholics, on the other hand, thought his views too easy-going, and censured him in the Index. The book, in fact, caused an uproar, and Lipsius, wearied with the struggle, with his conscience[16] troubled by the concessions he had to make to the Protestant party, applied for and obtained a six months' leave of absence, so that he might go to the Spa waters. He never returned to Leyden. Leaving Spa, he went to the Jesuits at Mayence, and that was the signal of his rupture with Holland (1591).

Offers and invitations poured in upon him—from Duke William of Bohemia, from the Bishop of Cologne, from the King of France (Henri IV.), from Pope Clement VIII., from the Senate of Venice, from the Universities of Padua, Bologna, etc. These offers he refused, partly from love of independence, partly from a sense of physical[17] and moral

---

[16] Zanta.

[17] After 1591 he seems to have suffered a good deal from some liver complaint.

lassitude, but chiefly, perhaps, from the favourable prospects held out by the Jesuits of a chair at the Catholic University of Louvain. Zanta suggests, even, that to the Jesuits may be attributed the rupture with Leyden.[18] Lipsius accepted the Chair of Latin History and Literature at Louvain in 1592. At this town he remained to the end of his life, teaching in the University, whose buildings and whose priceless library have now been so ruthlessly destroyed. His fame grew, and he had many pupils, who called themselves Lipsians. He finished his big work, *De militia romana*, in 1595. Then came the writing of his book, *Philosophia et physiologia Stoica*. During its progress—probably in 1602 or 1603—he had a severe illness, which lasted about six months. He refers to it in Part II., §§1, 2, saying that he had barely escaped death, and that now, though the disease had gone, it had left him languid and weak. This book he published in 1604. In 1605 came his folio edition of Seneca (without the plays); in 1606, *Monita et exempla politica*. At Louvain also he planned the publication of a vast collection of Belgian chronicles. His last years were troubled by further religious attacks from the Protestants. Those who are interested in the controversies, and in Lipsius' attitude to the matters involved, may see Van der Haeghen's *Bibliotheca Belgica*. Van der Haeghen, as the *Grande Encyclopédie* says, seems to have formed a right judgment concerning the changing religious opinions of the great Belgian philologist.[19]

Zanta's summary of the close of Lipsius' life, of his personal character, and of his place in the history of Stoicism (a place which Zanta, as already indicated, regards more especially from the Christian point of view), is well worth noting. It may be briefly stated as follows: The period at Louvain, he says, crowned Lipsius' career, and marked the complete development of his Stoicism. He could now in peace do his work as scholar, as philosopher, as guide and friend to pupils. He could gather together the materials

[18] P. 160 note.

[19] The *mot* of Antonius Musa, given in a little book entitled *Singularia de viris eruditione florentibus* (Wittenberg, 1728), *se non è vero, è molto ben trovato*. Referring to these variations and to the *De Constantia*, he thinks Lipsius was "scriptor de constantia inconstantissimus."

for his big final work on Seneca. To this end the *Manuductio ad Stoicam philosophiam* and the *Physiologia Stoicorum*
remain "comme une source précieuse de renseignements sur
l'état d'âme de leur auteur vis-à-vis des morales anciennes."
In March, 1606, he fell ill of pneumonia or pleurisy, and
foresaw that the attack would prove fatal. He summoned
his confessor, Léonard Lessius. A friend at his bedside
began to praise his stoical resignation, but Lipsius inter-
rupted him. "These things are vain," he said, and, pointing
to a crucifix, added simply, "there is the true patience."[20]
Lipsius was the restorer of Stoicism to the Renaissance—or,
rather, to be exact, the founder of Neo-Stoicism. Lipsius
appears, then, as a sage, but as a very human sage. Of the
antique virtue of the first Stoics, he preserved the moderation
and not the courage. He endured Fate's vicissitudes rather
than braved them. He suffered from them, yet would
willingly have found a remedy so as not to suffer from them.
That is the sentiment which inspired his *De Constantia*.
The special form of his Stoicism is attributable to three
things—temperament, practical conviction, and the education given him by the Jesuits, who were, be it remembered,
excellent humanists. Of weak health, he was by temperament not a fighter; he lacked the strength. He would rather
circumvent difficulties than meet them face to face. Life
had taught him, moreover, how often great sacrifices were
futile. If he had no taste for extreme poverty, for Epictetus'
"pallet and earthenware lamp," on the other hand he set
no store by riches and honours. He accepted duties which
enabled him to live. He refused conspicuous offices, such
as that of State Counsellor, which the Archduke Albert
offered him, knowing the envy they aroused. His Stoicism
took practical form first in his *De Constantia*. "This book,"
he said, comparing it with his other works, "I wrote chiefly
for myself, for my own well-being; the others I wrote for
my reputation." In it he assimilated Stoicism according
to his needs, making a first practical selection of the dogmas
which seemed salutary for him as a Christian humanist, a
friend of letters, a scholar driven from his native land by a
devastating civil war. Thus the definitive choice of Stoicism

[20] See Miræus' *Vita Justi Lipsii*.

was prepared which he made later, in a period which may be called that of his dogmatic Stoicism. In this second period he studied point by point, in his *Manuductio* and *Physiologia*, the Stoicism whose whole history he traced with the manifest aim of comparing it with the Christianity of the Bible and the Fathers of the Church.

Such, then, is Zanta's summary.

Lipsius issued many books on Latin authors and Roman life over and above those that have been mentioned. The full list of his publications is given in Van der Haeghen's *Bibliotheca Belgica*.

With regard to the *Autobiography*, which has been already mentioned, this was a letter written in 1600 to Woverius, a favourite pupil. Woverius had urged the making of the record, and Lipsius with apparent reluctance consented. It is Letter 87 in *Epistolarum selectarum centuria miscellanea* (1602). Bergmans, in 1889, edited it separately (Gand: Vanderhaeghen), giving a French translation and ample notes, and prefixing a portrait, in which Lipsius looks somewhat older than he does in the *Imagines Philologorum*, already referred to. The pamphlet is still readily procurable.

As to Lipsius' general reputation and high standing, the *Grande Encyclopédie* says: "The services rendered by J. Lipsius to philology and history are immense; there is hardly a problem relating to Roman antiquities on which his criticism has not thrown lasting light, and most of his treatises are models of depth and erudition. We resort to them even at the present day, and cannot deny him the glory of having given to literary and historical studies a fruitful and enduring impulse."

Much has often been said about Lipsius' religious changes and hesitations. It should perhaps be borne in mind, however, that he was primarily a humanist (as the long record of his publications shows) rather than a theologian. In matters of philosophy, as he himself says in effect in his book on Stoicism,[21] "neither a Plato nor an Aristotle should be exclusively followed, nor even one school only. If we call ourselves anything, it might be Eclectics." He was quick to recognise the good points in the various sects he

[21] I., §§4, 5.

studied.   Doubtless the same breadth of view characterised
his attitude towards Christian creeds.   Valuing the good in
each, the minuter network of their dogmas may well have
failed to appeal to him, or even have seemed to him a matter
of some indifference.   When it became somewhat urgent,
however, to make a definite choice, he sided finally with his
old friends and teachers the Jesuits.

What with his teaching, his controversies, and the long
list of books that he published, Lipsius was a very busy man.
From incidental distractions, too, he was no more immune
than other learned men are wont to be.   At one place in his
book on *Stoic Philosophy*,[22] where his pupil, coming to see
him very early, finds him already busy, he describes the
interruptions to which he is constantly liable; for his own
pursuits and for serious matters he seems only to have
broken oddments of time.   "I could almost aver, with
Livius Drusus," he says, "'that to me alone no holiday has
fallen, from boyhood up.'   I get up in the morning.   'Here
are letters; answer them.'   That done, I turn to other
things.   My servant comes to say that some nobleman has
called, or a youth from France, or Germany, or Sarmatia;
they wish to pay their respects.   The one and the other
want some token of my friendship inscribed in their albums.
I have hardly recovered breath when one of my Belgian
friends appears: 'So sorry to disturb you, but I've written
a poem—or a pamphlet—and I want you to read it.'
'Anything further?'   'Criticise it and correct it.'   'What
else?'   'Just write some preliminary verses or commenda-
tion.'   Then I think I'm really free; but someone else turns
up and wants an epitaph, either for himself or his brother
or his father or a friend, or else an inscription for a house
or a citadel or an altar.   Then what about my students—
like yourself?   You know how readily they have access to
me, and how I listen to them, answer them, direct them,
and set them in what I believe to be the right way of study.
This is the one sort of work that I least regret amongst all
the others.   It makes little difference whether I help them
by talking or by writing, except that in one case perhaps
more hear me, whilst in the other, although fewer receive

[22] Part II., Book III., §1.

what I say, yet perhaps the result is more effective and fruitful. So my life is spent, and I learn to put up with it; patience lightens the burden which our shoulders must needs bear. . . . Still, from time to time I return to myself, and can turn over in my mind something healthful and profitable to myself—a little superficially perhaps, and incidentally; yet I do turn it over."

This account of Lipsius' life, and of his outlook on life, may perhaps suffice.

As to the estimation in which he has been generally held, both by contemporaries and by later critics, certain important judgments and significant facts have already been given. Reference has been made, for instance, to the views of modern writers like Zanta and Hubert. In his own day, there was the eagerness with which many Universities and great rulers sought to win him to their own precincts or their own courts; but there were also the bitter attacks that were made upon him. Opinions about him, in fact, have been conflicting; he has had keen partisans and equally keen depreciators. Among his contemporaries, whilst many admired him greatly, others, such as H. Stephanus and Joseph Scaliger, roughly assailed and belittled him; apparently scholars' rivalry and *odium theologicum* influenced them. Sagittarius, too, was another foe. That Lipsius was a force to reckon with, that he was one of the outstanding figures of his time, seems proved by the very bitterness of their attacks. Then in recent days the view of Nisard, in the work already cited, is noteworthy. His general estimate is high, though he does not fail to draw attention to what he regards as defects in character and taste. Perhaps, indeed, he over-emphasizes them: they were partly the manners of the age; and in any case it is given to few men to live for sixty years *sans peur et sans reproche*. He thinks his character, whilst sweet and amiable, often showed an undue facility and a lack of strength. The following passage will show how he places Lipsius historically. It is taken from the first chapter of his *Triumvirat Littéraire*. After referring to an earlier triumvirate of the sixteenth century—Erasmus, Melanchthon, Joachim Camerarius—he says: "These three illustrious men had hardly concluded the first fifty or sixty years of the sixteenth century, when three others equally illustrious—viz., Joseph Scaliger, Justus Lipsius, and Isaac Casaubon—were born, and in the second half of the century came to occupy the glorious place which their predecessors had held in the first half. The juxtaposition which I make of this double triumvirate is not arbitrary; it is neither the result of caprice nor of a personal taste for analogies; it is sufficiently indicated by the facts. Erasmus, Melanchthon, and Camerarius, have all three exercised, by their writings, an equal and simultaneous influence on the study of Letters, properly so called, in Germany; and if they did not obtain from their contemporaries the *title* of a triumvirate, they nevertheless exercised its *authority*. But Lipsius, Scaliger, and Casaubon, had alike its power and its name. In their time Learning, as it grew more refined, grew also more pedantic; therefore, in submitting to the laws of the three critics who were then its own highest expression, it scrupulously gave them, in the Republic of Letters, a title which proudly voiced their authority and their number. Thus it was that Justus Lipsius, Joseph Scaliger, and Isaac Casaubon, ·had the designation of *Literary Triumvirate* conferred upon them."

Nisard concludes his work on Lipsius thus: "Any nation might be proud of having such a man as Lipsius for its compatriot; any nation might think itself honoured in rendering him some conspicuous homage to perpetuate the *scholar's* glory and the *nation's* gratitude. Nevertheless, while the *place publique* of Rotterdam proudly exhibits the statue of Erasmus, the *place publique* of Louvain is still waiting for the statue of Lipsius."

Let us now turn to Lipsius' book on Stoicism, which was published, as I have said, in 1604. In my own edition (that of 1644) the whole title-page is engraved, and its illustration shows the interior of a stone building, with doorways and pillars, and seven grown men. The central figure is probably Lipsius himself (at least, it bears some resemblance to his likeness), and he is speaking, possibly on Stoicism, to some of the others. In the book itself, however, he has only one interlocutor—a youth.

Expressed in outline, the first part is as follows: After a
general exhortation to the study of philosophy in preference
to that simply of elegant, or entertaining, or practical arts
(which, however, form a useful preliminary training of the
mind), Lipsius comes to the question, From whom should
we seek our philosophy?   Neither a Plato nor an Aristotle
should be exclusively followed, nor even one school only.
If we call ourselves anything, it might be Eclectics.   In
order to exhibit what is the field of selection, Lipsius runs
over the main schools that have existed—the Barbarian,
the Italian, and more especially the Greek.

Having thus cleared the ground, he shows the origin and
succession of the Stoic school, from the Cynics down to
Seneca. To the founder of Stoicism, Zeno of Citium, and
to his life, he of course gives prominence, and then passes
on to Cleanthes, Chrysippus, Zeno of Sidon, Diogenes called
the Babylonian, Antipater of Sidon, Panætius, Posidonius,
etc. To the Cynics, at their best, and in essentials, he gives
high praise; and he records some of their views, on which
certain Stoic doctrines and paradoxes were founded. He
then states, and answers, several customary objections to
Stoicism, and *per contra* sings its praise, showing in what
parts of philosophy Stoics have excelled, and naming as
examples certain great Stoics, among the rest Seneca and
Epictetus.

What are the parts and definitions of philosophy? One
broad division is into Contemplative and Active. Another
is that of Seneca—viz., into Moral, Natural, and Rational.
The meanings assigned to these terms and divisions are
discussed, and also their several importance and value,
Ethics being ranked as the foremost in fruitfulness. Coming
then to the distinction between Philosophy and Wisdom,
Lipsius shows that it is similar to that between the end and
the means; or to that between the perfect good of the human
mind, and the love and pursuit of that good. The perfect
Wise Man of the Stoics is not found, but is an ideal only;
the man, however, who is in a *state of progress* towards
Wisdom does exist. Wisdom, in the Stoic view, may be
taught; and Lipsius gives the Stoic theory of Knowledge.
The mind receives appearances (*phantasiæ* or *visa*), and is

impressed or affected by them (whence the τύπωσις of
Zeno, the ἀλλοίωσις or ἑτεροίωσις of Chrysippus). The
more lasting of these perceptions give rise to memory;
repeated acts of memory to experience. Hence arise conceptions of things. Then come reason and ratiocination,
and so at last knowledge and wisdom. The Object or End
that is pursued is, for Stoics, the living according to Nature.
This has been understood in somewhat different fashions,
and the views of Zeno, Cleanthes, and Chrysippus, are
shown in their gradual development from vagueness into
clearness. Living according to Nature came to mean living
according to right reason, or according to Virtue, and hence
to mean seeking after God, who becomes the all-important
Object or End. Hence Virtue alone is sufficient for happiness, and no outward goods or gifts of fortune are needful.
If it is suggested that external goods (like health, strength,
etc.), being in accordance with Nature, conduce to the
practice of Virtue, the stricter Stoics would reply that they
recognise no good things, and no evil things, save those of
the mind. The Stoic division and classification of things
that are good are next given, and are followed by the Stoic
account of things neutral (or indifferent).

By way of introduction to the next division, Lipsius urges
that we should arm ourselves against the anxieties of the
world—its fears and hopes—by studying philosophy, and by
having always in mind the Stoic Decrees (or Ordinances or
Axioms). These *Decreta* are like the root, the trunk, and
the branches, of a tree. The first of them (or the root) was
the recognition of the Object or End described above.
The second (or trunk) was the understanding of the nature of
the Good, also defined and classified. The third (or rami-
fication) comprises those decrees that are common to most
schools of philosophy, as well as those that are special to the
Stoics—viz., the Paradoxes. It is with these that Lipsius
is now concerned, and he treats a number of them separately,
—e.g. The Wise man is of constant and equable mind, and is
always happy; The Wise man is happy even when in tor-
ments; The Wise man is imperturbable and free from excessive passions (this is the famous ἀπάθεια); etc.

In the second part of the book we come to the Stoic

Physiologia, or Physics. It comprises things above, around, and below us—the whole universe, in fact, and all that it contains—God, Genii, Men. The two main divisions of the subject are the Corporeal and the Incorporeal. The Corporeal comprises *Principia* (or the things which produce or make), and *Elementa* (or things that are produced, and what springs therefrom). The Incorporeals are space, time, etc. Following Seneca, Lipsius begins with the *Principia*. These are twofold—God (the active), and Matter (the passive). These two principia are called "Natures." The word "Nature," then, to the Stoic includes God and Divine Reason permeating the whole world and its parts; and they define Nature as a fire. This fire is generative and constructive and preservative, and its work is that of a reasoning artificer. God, according to the Stoics, is also the world itself; He is One, Good, Provident. This unity, this goodness, and this watchful providence (both for the universe and for individuals), are next discussed. In providence or foresight the idea of Fate is involved, this Fate being described as the reason, or method, according to which the world is administered. Chrysippus interprets Fate as the truth, the nature, and the necessity, of things.

Various objections are then considered against God's providence and goodness, and. the inquiry, *Whence come natural or external evils?* is examined first. By natural evils are understood monsters and prodigies, poisons and evil beasts. Then a second inquiry, *Whence come internal evils, or sin?* is examined. Here the Stoic view is that, although God has given man powers and faculties which, by certain applications, may be employed to commit sin, yet it is by our own act and will that they are actually so applied. If our natural constitution provokes this wrong choice, then the first defect lies in nature, or the material of which we are made. The origin of evil, in fact, both internal and external, is placed, not in God, but in Matter (which is coeval with Him and eternal). Of course, too, many so-called evils, such as poverty, pain, etc., are in the Stoic view not evils at all. With regard to God's toleration of our wrong-doing, He may foresee or see things, without fore-ordaining or causing them. Man's choice must be left free if he is to approach perfection or be more than an automaton.

The next division is begun after a break of six months, during which Lipsius has had a dangerous illness. He comes now to the other Stoic division of the Principia—viz., Matter. It is twofold—Universal and Particular. The Universal neither waxes nor wanes; the Particular both waxes and wanes. Matter is eternal, and is corporeal. It can suffer change, since it can take different forms (in the Particular) and can be infinitely subdivided. All things that exist are to the Stoics bodies: God, Matter, Virtues, Vices, Passions, Qualities, and so on—all are bodies. Lipsius then comes to the World (Mundus), which is the greatest and noblest of the Bodies. In Stoic phrase it includes the heavens, the earth, and God, and is the equivalent of Rerum Natura or Communis Natura. It may consist of either formed or unformed material. It differs from the Universe, which includes empty space (vacuum); whereas the World does not include empty space, but is contained in it. It was made by God, who changed all existence first into air, then into water (or moisture), and so into the mingled elements—fire, water, air, and earth. The World is animate, a living thing, endowed with sense and reason. The elements of which it is built up having been treated separately (Fire, Air, Water, and Earth), Lipsius considers the world (Mundus) as a whole. It is spoken of in two senses—either as consisting of all Nature (in which sense it is eternal), or as the ordered World (in which sense it is periodically destroyed and renewed, and is not eternal). In the latter sense it is liable to destruction both by water—the cataclysm —and by fire—the conflagration. That by water affects only the earth with all its life; but life will thereafter begin again, and the old order be renewed. The greater destruction (or rather change) by fire is, however, universal. It occurs when the Great Year (magnus annus) arrives, and thereafter a redintegration of all things is made. The time, the manner, and the purpose, of this destruction and renovation are discussed. A chapter is added in which the Incorporeals— Motion, Space, and Time—are touched upon.

Lipsius' next subject is the knowledge of man's nature and

mind. On the physical side, he gives the Stoic view of man's first origin and subsequent reproduction. A body having been produced, the soul itself is insinuated from without, after birth. The soul comes from the eternal fire, from God Himself, and is thus part of the universal soul that is diffused throughout the world. As to its immortality, Stoics speak doubtfully. On the whole they regard it as enduring for a long time, though not to eternity. At the great conflagration all souls are reabsorbed into the ethereal fire. Some held—e.g. Chrysippus—that only the wise endured so long; the evil perished sooner.

The various divisions of the soul are then indicated; and finally Lipsius discusses the principal part of the soul (ἡγεμονικόν, the Principale of Seneca, the Principatus of Cicero). It is that which imagines, assents, perceives, desires. With a few final words on the dignity of the soul, Lipsius closes his book.

Such, then, is the subject-matter of this book on Stoicism. In the course of his work Lipsius quotes from a great number of authors, partly for the purpose of direct exposition, partly for illustration and embellishment. As is indicated by the title-page, Seneca's writings are of especial value to him. Among these, the Epistles and the Dialogues stand out conspicuous, though the *Quæstiones Naturales* and other writings are freely used. Quotations from Cicero, also, as one would expect, are abundant, especially from the *De Officiis*, Tusculan Disputations, *De Finibus*, *De Natura Deorum*, *Quæstiones Academicæ*. Diogenes Laertius, of course, makes his appearance everywhere. After these, perhaps Plato and Plutarch are cited the most; nor is Aristotle neglected. Of Plutarch's works, the most frequently quoted are, perhaps, *De Placitis Philosophorum*, *Adversus Stoicos*, and *De Communibus Notionibus*. Others, however (such as *Quæstiones Conviviales*, *Quæstiones Platonicæ*), are also often requisitioned. Naturally, Epictetus is much in evidence; but Marcus Aurelius is found less often than one might have expected. The Scriptures are frequently quoted, so also are many of the Fathers of the Church. But the list is too long and too varied to give here. Suffice it to say that, besides the names mentioned, I have noted thirty-four others, and there still remain those not noted. That he gathered his materials from such diverse sources has been made a reproach to Lipsius; and Nisard is among his critics. Into certain writers, indeed, apart from his use of them for happy illustration, he does read Stoicism unnecessarily. Views which are the common property of mankind, and which, therefore, are also found in Stoicism, he sometimes quotes as showing that one man or another has Stoic leanings. Yet even the expansiveness of his methods, and the wide field he covered in seeking his materials, have their interest to those who for the nonce are not hurried in their reading, but can afford to go leisurably. It is a method that at least helps to remind one how close is often the relation between different schools of thought, and how many of the world's ideas are a possession held by all the schools.

The general contents of his book on Stoicism having been given, certain characteristics that illustrate Lipsius' tastes and style may now be touched upon. The Latin in which the work is written is often eloquent; it is free from superfluity, and, though here and there compact to the verge of obscurity, it is for the most part clear. Nisard (*Le Triumvirat*, p. 140 *et seq.*) gives on this subject some valuable pages, in which he speaks of Lipsius' departure from Ciceronian canons, and his delight in a more piquant Atticism;[23] his power of subtle brevity, and yet of full eloquence;[24] his use, and perhaps his abuse, of old words. He gives also an account of the disordered and broken style into which his scholars and imitators (the Lipsians) fell, through copying mannerisms which they, lacking the needful genius and learning, could not use with success. Hence Lipsius advised them, instead of imitating himself, to take Cicero's more natural style as their model. The passage is well worth perusal, and perhaps explains the disrepute into which the adjective "Lipsian," as applied to compositions, seems to have fallen before it became obsolete (as Webster now

[23] "Si, comme il cherchait à se le persuader et à le persuader aux autres Lipse aima toujours Cicéron, il cessa bientôt de l'imiter, avouant qu'il trouvait plus de charmes au piquant de l'atticisme, qu'à la délicatesse asiatique qui est le fond du style de Cicéron" (pp. 140–141). Nisard thinks that Lipsius came, in particular, under the spell of Plautus, Sallust, Tacitus, the two Senecas, and even Apuleius.

[24] Nisard's comments remind one of Lipsius' own description of Seneca's style. See the note concluding this article.

describes it). Looking at another aspect of Lipsius, one recognises the care of the scholar in the innumerable references he gives in the margin of the text; one finds it, too, in his frequent critical emendations of obscure or corrupt passages. As to his interlocutor (a pupil), one would not say much; he is a lay figure, a "man of straw," who, while giving a certain variety to the composition, and expressing opinions which Lipsius may combat and demolish, is in himself not personally interesting, and has but small dramatic value. It is Lipsius' own exposition that chiefly attracts one; and in it one relishes the ample and leisurely progress with which the argument is carried forward, and the fulness with which the points that arise are illustrated. His frequent little perorations, too, as he reaches stage after stage, are welcome and enjoyable.[25] The whole work reveals in Lipsius wide reading, scholarly aims, and love of virtue. If at times, in his dealing with pagan writings and creeds and philosophies, he appears at curious pains to avow his Christianity, one remembers, after all, that he lived, as regards matters of religion, in a most restless and censorious age. Though he himself was quick to recognise moral excellence in many of the old ways of thought, yet he knew from experience how bitter the men of his own generation could be.

In Seneca, as is already apparent, Lipsius found perpetual delight; his innumerable quotations, and, indeed, the very title-page of the work, attest the enthusiasm he felt. He admired his literary style, and conceived his personal character to be of rare nobility and charm. In some eloquent pages he summarises the notable features of the one, and gives an *apologia* and a defence of the other. Considerations of space, however, make it impossible to offer a translation of these passages. They will be found in Book I., § 18. One is appended to this article.

A valuable clue to a man's own ideals and aspirations is obtained by observing the things and the qualities which he spontaneously praises. They show "which way the wind

[25] One would, indeed, greet cordially a reprint of this and other writings by Lipsius, produced in a clear type, and with the references to the authors he quotes adjusted to modern editions.

blows," just as an artist's special bent is revealed by the kind of pictures he paints of his own free choice. To the view of Lipsius' character, therefore, which we have already formed, confirmation may be added by considering the high-minded Seneca whom he presents to us—whether that character is in part an ideal creation, or is indeed the veritable Seneca of history. We shall think of Lipsius, then, as a man of lofty aims, of broad and generous judgment, zealous for the welfare of those with whom he is associated, free from avarice and ostentation, devoted to learning, fain of a simple and virtuous life. As to Seneca himself, it is true that Lipsius ranked both his life and character higher than a good many scholars rank them now. Yet even if, in his eulogy and vindication, he fails to carry all modern readers the whole way with him, his judgment and his attitude, which are interesting in themselves, may at least give one pause. They are the views of a close student of Seneca, and of a famous scholar and teacher, who left his mark on a great University. The outward glory of that University, alas! is departed: its buildings are shattered, its library of priceless books and manuscripts charred to shreds and fragments, its portraits—Lipsius, Erasmus, Jansen (Bishop of Ypres), Vesalius (the anatomist), Puteanus (pupil and successor of Lipsius at Louvain)—all are hopelessly gone. Yet the history of that University's thought can be still kept in remembrance. The body indeed is dead, but the spirit may still live.

The following criticism of Seneca's style is interesting. The Latin, too, which follows it, will serve as a brief example of Lipsius' own style. The passage is from Book I., §18, p. 103 (1644 edition):

"His words are choice, suitable and significant; they always mean something more than they actually say. And this seems a special genius of his, that in an economy of words he has a wonderful force and efficacy; in brevity he has clearness and brilliance. Allusions, figures, metaphors, are frequent, almost continuous; and these both please and instruct, directing the mind to the subject, and even beyond the subject. There is carefulness without affectation; ornament without finery (*comptus*);

there is close arrangement in what he says, but nothing forced or crabbed. Style also is apparent, and virile harmony and rhythm, yet in such a way that, while you recognise artistic construction, you will admit no effeminate artificiality, and it is for fighting and the arena that the whole equipment is made, not for pleasure and scenic show. Then, too, in his very brevity and terseness of speech there is manifest a certain happy abundance : his words well forth amply, though not wastefully; they flow, not rush; they are like a river, not a torrent; they move on with strength, but without spate. Lastly, like goodly trees that, whilst their chief property is to bear fruit, have yet flowers and leaves: so Seneca, whom for his fruit's sake we read and admire, brings us delight at the same time, putting Venus beside Minerva."

(An ex vero, aut affectu sic iudicem, vide. Tria sunt, quæ huc me ducunt, Verba, Res, Tractatus: omnia in eo iure laudanda. Verba, selecta, propria, significantia: immo quæ plus aliquid semper dicunt, quam dicunt. Qui proprius quidam eius Genius videtur, ut in parcimonia verborum mira ἐνέργεια atque efficacia sit; in brevitate, claritas et splendor. Sunt allusiones, imagines, translationes, crebræ et pæne continuæ: quæ delectant simul et docent; et in rem animum, atque extra rem mittunt. Est cura, non affectatio; decor, non comptus; tractata oratio, non torta. Est et compositio quædam et viriles numeri: sed ut structuram agnoscas, mollitiem abnuas; et pugnæ atque arenæ omnia, non delectationi aut scænæ parata. Iam in ipsa brevitate, et stricto dicendi genere, apparet beata quædam copia. Fundit verba, etsi non effundit; fluit, non rapitur; amni similis, torrenti dissimilis; cum impetu, sed sine perturbatione se ferens. Denique, ut felices arbores, quarum præcipua dos est fructum ferre, flores et folia tamen habent: sic iste, quem fructus caussa legimus et colimus, oblectationem adfert pariter, et Venerem cum Minerva iungit.)

In Northumbrian Sunshine

As I approached Warkworth on a summer's evening from the station, I saw afar, as if self-supported on a grey misty background of blending sea and sky, a building that gleamed like brilliant marble. It was the lighthouse of Coquet Island. The sun, though powerless to dispel the far-spread outer mist, had at least captured this white outpost, and had blazoned upon its walls his seal of possession. I saw also the upstanding towers of Warkworth Castle, duller in tone, but conspicuously reared on the summit of the hill. When I had reached the river Coquet, crossed the ancient bridge, and passed through its massive gateway, the village itself was before me. It rises clean and grey, with patches of red roofs, up the steep road to the castle foot. Then the great keep springs aloft, and the ruined walls. Customarily they are yellow-grey and sober of tint; though once, after a long day of rain and gloom, I have seen them under a new aspect. By some vehement outflaming of sunset light the broken towers were turned to living crimson against the half-illumined purple background, and the walls changed into golden fire: their patient strength of the earth was transfigured, and was mated with the splendours of the sky.

On sunny mornings, down by the winding river-side, one will come upon many a charming sight. Here below the bridge are three fishermen netting salmon. Two are in the water holding one end of the net; their mate slowly lets out its full length from the boat as he rows first upstream and then back in a broad curve. He joins the others, and the three haul it in again. Sometimes it comes in empty, but often the gathering folds are well filled with fish. A blow to each with a short stick, and they may be grasped and tossed like bars of gleaming silver into the boat. I turn from this to the solitude above the bridge. Here are ·upstanding boulders and moss-grown slabs of rock, or, when the water is low, ribbed sand and gravelly bottom and green trailing weeds. Fish, all in freedom here, leap out and splash in again, and the rippling circles widen and spread to either bank. As the pulse of the incoming tide is felt, undulations curve up against the stream and the volume of the water gradually swells; a current is seen flowing upwards, till the sand and lower rocks are covered and the banks grow full. Even in times of grey rain and in rough winds the tree-girt river has its beauties, its play of light and shade, its dim reflections that sweep over the wind-brushed surface deep into the gloomier shadows of trees and grassy banks. But now in blazing sunshine, and when the wind is still, the scene is indeed a lovely one. The unruffled water, as it curves silently away beneath the trees, is full of colour, is a miracle of reflections, clear as in a still lake. The colour and the form of the green trees, of the broad-leaved coltsfoot at the water's edge, and of the meadow-grass, are repeated; the dull yellow of the earth-banks is also answered, along with the vivid yellow of the ragwort, the blue of the sky, and the gleam of fleecy clouds. There, too, under the water, dances a phantom white butterfly; or a mimic sea-gull wings its leisurely white way up-stream, questing for food. Under a light stir of air, a minute and flickering net-work is spun swiftly over the relucent surface; or rippling wavelets, like the ribbed sand left bare at the margin, are briefly seen. Then all grows still again, and the magic of the mirror is restored.

Nor, apart from these riches of its natural beauty, is the Coquet poor in long annals of human experience. Was it not, in the old days of swift raids and assaults and warfare, a first barrier of safety against the foe; engirdling as it does on three sides the hill on which are set the clustering houses, and the great castle that formed their last defence? The romance too of Bertram's Hermitage, down on the river's bank, cannot be forgotten—a long-enduring love, a stormy tragedy, and at the last resignation and simple hermit-piety. What of that grim and battered giant's face, again, which, through a break in the foliage, one may descry protruding from the rock near the Hermit's cell? Huge and ugly, with one eye crushed violently in, it glares from amidst the trees ever balefully towards the castle. Is it fashioned merely by slow action of frost and wind and rain? Or is it not in truth some legendary monster imprisoned there in his frozen hatred by an enduring spell of wizardry? Through the mist of centuries these "old, unhappy, far-off things" surge into renewed life. Anon they again fade away, even as, in the obscuring fogs that at times creep over the countryside as evening falls, roads and green fields are merged into a stretch of grey vapour, fences are blotted out, and the trunks of trees are hidden, so that only their branches and foliage are seen, unstayed and fantastic against the sky. Of the castle, too, the foundations are obliterated, and the upper walls and the towers rise gaunt and grey into the night.

That changeful mystery of a closing day has its romance and its charm. Yet actually the beauty of the twilight is perhaps greater when seen unveiled and clear. As I go up through the village I see the full golden moon at first beyond the dusky ruins of the castle. Presently, where a fringe of trees skirts the edge of the hill, her glimpses may be caught through their foliage, whilst down in the valley in the clear interspaces of the tree-trunks her flashings and long reflections are seen upon the expanse of the river's broad bosom. Passing into the open country I watch her, at first regal and solitary in a wide blue domain, then queening it radiantly above the light clouds that, as it were in their obeisance, are enkindled and beautified. Anon I turn aside into a field-path, where through the lattice-work of leafy hedge-rows her lovely brilliance is again intercepted. But the path changes its course and leads away from her, and I walk for a while through fields all dim and grey till the corner of the castle grounds is reached, and the edge of the wooded banks that slope down steeply to the river. The shoulder of the hill, as I descend the steps cut in it, shuts the moon finally away from me, and I see her no more. Yet instead I find another scene of twilight wonderland; for, still faintly illuminated with the pale afterglow of sunset, the further bank bends forward, approaching the river in a great horse-shoe, here wan with yellow corn, there dark with grass-fields. The blue and grey sky is broken by many clouds. The curving water, which beneath the shadow of the trees runs black, is in the open patches luminous with faint silvery reflections.

Outside Warkworth itself there are other scenes which, once beheld, remain in remembrance. In the August sunshine we ride one afternoon northwards, out from the cool deep grove of lofty trees beyond the bridge, into the open blaze of light and heat, on past fields of golden barley margining the blue misty sea, until presently, away beyond the grassy dunes, we descry, set on a sloping promontory's low point, the huddle of red houses that is Alnmouth. Soon the winding river grows distinct, with its white boats decked with sails brown or white; then to the right the gleaming line of breakers, and beyond them the wide unbroken sapphire of the sea. The quiet greys and browns, too, of other houses in the village become clear, and the church spire catches the eye. We linger on the long bridge, till in the evening light the peaceful river becomes overspread with a sheen like mother-of-pearl—a delicate, living marvel of grey and palest pink and blue.

Or perchance some evening we follow the winding lanes that rise and fall westwards to Morwick Mill. There, down in the river bed, the bold red cliff, the clumped foliage of the neighbouring trees—sycamore and Scotch fir—and in the foreground the cows standing in the cool water after the hot day, make a scene such as Bewick would have loved to engrave. All is quiet and secluded, and the evening air is clear; around us are hills and curving valleys, trees and grassy mounds. Presently, as we turn homewards again, a grey mist comes up the river-bed. It swells above the banks and spreads fast over the adjacent slopes, veiling the whole countryside with its heavy moisture. The parched hedges and trees drink it in and are once more refreshed.

Often too we are drawn to the neighbourhood of Guyzance, which we chiefly love to approach from the south, by way of Acklington village, with its little cottage-gardens deeply overgrown with white and red phlox and many another flower, and with its pretty red-roofed well. From there the road soon drops down to the Coquet, where on a

sunny day the lovely light-filled reach of smooth water
will entrance us as we watch the leaping fish, and the water-
fowl that swim from bank to bank, to and fro, across the
river, or catch sight of a heron flying slowly down-stream
into the distance. Below the bridge an angler is wading,
busy at his sport. A little further on, the road brings us to
a cool grove of trees, harbouring and overarching moist
rocky dells all filled with ferns and delightful greenery.

Wanting wider horizons some other day, I start riding
with a friend, in lowering weather, away towards the south-
west. Leaving Acklington and its gardens, we head towards
Felton. Soon the country opens out and distant hills are
seen; but these, which a few evenings since, in the sunset
light, were luminous with changeful greys and rich purples,
are now black and thunderous, portending troubled faring
to cyclists. We drop swiftly down on Felton, a village
charmingly placed at the meeting of the great North Road
and the river. Though it is now, since the coming of the
motor-cars, less tranquil than in bygone years, yet the
curving road, the stone bridge, the trout-filled Coquet, the
many trees and the encompassing hills still compel one to a
lingering. One recalls the old delights of the place, and not
least that sheltered spot, not far upstream, where, within
the thick leafy screen of the banks, was a deep pool: there,
on a midsummer day, a gleaming plunge and a few strokes
of swimming once brought swift joy and cooling refreshment
after the blazing sunshine. For us to-day, however, there
can be but a brief pause here. The postmistress, standing
outside her shop, points out our road; she thinks that, in
spite of the ominous clouds, prospects are not amiss. So
we pass on towards Swarland, into the heart of the north-
west wind. Blacker and gloomier grows the sky, and soon
a few drops of rain fall, which must surely be the prelude,
we think, to the battering deluge of a thunderstorm. Shall
one turn back forthwith and run for home, or stop in the
hamlet for shelter, or, "come what come may," still hold
steadily on into the open country? My comrade, loth to
break a plan once made, votes for the advance, and we press
on, up and down, amidst the hills. The drops of rain cease.
Ere long, as we approach Longframlington, an edging of

lighter grey appears below the clouds on the horizon, and soon, as if somewhere the sun were struggling to come forth, I can discern even a faint shadow or two. When Long-framlington is passed, there is a swinging descent to the Coquet valley: then our road, turning up-stream, runs through Pauperhaugh north-west towards Rothbury, the beauty of the approach enhanced by gleams of sunshine, by the running water, and by the densely wooded hillside. On the way we meet hundreds of sheep, returning with their shepherds from a fruitless market; trouble on the railway, we learn, has made transport of the flocks impossible, and they must be driven home again, faring toilsomely back to their pastures. At Rothbury we lunch, and then saunter for a while round the village, and across the stepping-stones. By now the day has entirely cleared, the sun shines cheerily, and there is no further risk of rain. We get gladly to saddle again, and start northwards along the road to Alnwick. But the ascent soon becomes too steep for riding, and we must walk. We go past fir woods, rich with resinous perfume, till we are well round the shoulder of the hill that hides the village; we pause now and again and look back with delight at the dark wooded slopes and, in the background, the fine mass of seven-ridged Simonside. Rising steadily higher, we get here and there a brief ride, where there is a dip in the road. We still overtake flocks of sheep dispersing from that futile fair. At last, reaching the top, 900 feet above the sea, we emerge on the open moorland and catch the aromatic, honey-laden smell of wide-stretching, sun-filled heather. Ah, the deep joyous breaths we draw, till our lungs are like to crack! To the left the land falls slowly away, so that ridge after ridge of the Cheviots is revealed in the purple distance. We glide down the long descent; we skirt Edlingham, which lies below us on the left, with its old church and ruined castle, and admire the bold elliptic curve of the railway that comes from Glanton and Wooler in the north-west, then sweeps off to Alnwick in the north east. Another long climb, and we are upon Alnwick Moor; and then at last comes the welcome run down into Alnwick itself, through scenery that changes now, on these eastern slopes, to something more homely and agricultural:

we are again amidst farm-lands. At Alnwick we rest awhile, then stroll about looking at the old castle and streets and inscriptions; and thereafter ride easily and quietly homewards, past Lesbury, and over the adjacent bridge set in its deep grove of trees, onwards till we come within view of Alnmouth and the lightsome expanse of its river. Finally the brilliant lighthouse of Coquet Island, and then Warkworth Castle itself, are once more in sight.

Other days bring yet other delights. There are peaceful hours to spend amongst books, unharassed in this quiet village by vexing interruptions. Down by the sea, also, we can bask at ease on the hot sand, and bathe beneath a mid-day sun in cool blue waters.

In such fashion are the gathering pictures woven gradually into the fabric of memory; and presently, when we return to the busy scenes of ordinary life, the time of tranquil holiday being done, we shall often in swift thought revisit this fair neighbourhood: we shall see once more the winding river, the clean grey village, the stately ruins of the castle, and that distant beckoning vision of a radiant lighthouse.

The Lure of Translation[1]

I.

I WAS once showing to a journalistic friend of mine a copy of the late A. T. Barton's translation of Shakespeare's Sonnets into Latin verse. The book was issued, you may remember, in 1913 by some of Barton's pupils as a tribute to his memory. My friend, after admiring the get-up of the book (it is printed by the Riccardi Press) and looking at the portrait of Barton, which I have inserted, turned to me, and, laughing at the quip, said, "Why did the old man go spinning this cocoon about himself?" His pat journalist's question set me thinking in two directions. In the first place the mere putting of it implied, one would judge, some disesteem of the translator's art. To my friend, pre-occupied as he was with national problems and foreign relations—it was shortly before the war—the doing of such work may have seemed like a lapping in "soft Lydian airs," like fiddling while Rome burned. He may, again, have regarded such writing as imitative only, and unoriginal; and, whilst undervaluing the uses of such scholarship, also have underestimated, through insufficient classical knowledge, the rigours of toil involved. But in the second place, apart from this personal aspect of the matter, his question set me looking for a direct and appropriate answer. Why *do* these versions come into existence? What *is* the lure that calls them forth?

It will be serviceable, in order to understand the outlook and motives of translators, to examine the different kinds of work they produce. I propose, then, in the first place, to indicate some of the main groups into which translations fall, and to give various examples. Afterwards I shall return to the question of motives, and to a summary inquiry into the nature of translation as compared with other arts.

[1] A paper read to the Northumberland and Durham Classical Association in February, 1920.

The kinds of translation are numerous, though it is at times hard to say by what gradations one merges into another. Let us begin at the most elementary.

(1) There is the sedulous translation, possessing little or no literary merit. This kind has much in common with the bald crib issued for the use of "studious" youth.

(2) There are the translations which follow much of the text closely, but manipulate things in a way suitable for the simple reader and for "lasses and lads," omitting or slurring over defects of taste and opinions that are un-conventional.

(3) There are the broadly serviceable renderings which answer the purposes of an adult public concerned with the general sense mainly, and not careful about accuracy of detail. Literary form may well be present of course, some-times to a notable degree.

(4) There are the translations which make undeniably good literature, and are in many respects scholarly, but which, inasmuch as they have a way of evading the crux of a difficulty, disappoint careful students.

(5) There are the austere versions of trained scholars who to each point in the original, whether of fact or phrase or word-order or rhythm, endeavour to give unflinchingly the response of the new language, nothing extenuating, nothing embellishing or augmenting, but presenting truly the exact thoughts and meaning of the text.

(6) There is the expansive or explanatory translation, which as it goes along amplifies and comments upon the original. With this kind may be grouped, as an inferior species, the versions into which stock epithets, tags, and other gratuitous flourishes are introduced by the translator.

(7) There is the translation which we prize as if it were an original work of art. We admire it both as a most skilful version, and, in addition, for its own independent vitality and beauty. While it is closely allied to the austere translation mentioned above, it is perhaps a little freer and more vernacular. It is like a delightful flower on translation's formal plant.

(8) There are the adaptations. These are renderings which, sometimes possessing academic value, often belonging

to *Belles Lettres* of less restricted standards, give in picturesque equivalents rather than in literal closeness the sense of the original, and do not hesitate to change the images and allusions so as to suit a new medium and altered conditions.

(9) There is the paraphrase, which renders the spirit of the original more or less carefully, whilst professing no strict adherence to its words. It is perhaps more independent, and runs with a slacker rein, than the adaptation, which, as its name implies, is *fitted to* particular conditions. The two however have much in common, and the terms—adaptation, imitation, and paraphrase—are somewhat loosely employed.

(10) There is the parody. This, as the word indicates, is somewhat similar to the paraphrase, but it gives a mocking or burlesque twist to the original. In the skin of a lion an ass is exhibited.

(11) There is the impressionistic rendering, which, tied by no verbal bonds whatever, uses the original merely as a foothold whence it can spring forth *totus, teres atque rotundus*.

Some examples will serve to illustrate these groups, which are sufficiently comprehensive for my purpose.

(1) Examples of the unimaginative first kind—what Professor Phillimore calls "crib-lingo"—come quickly to the mind. You remember, for instance, the translation of the Aeneid in Bohn's Library—say the 4th Book, where Aeneas and Dido have their parting scene. Aeneas says: "That you, O queen, have laid me under numerous obligations, which you may recount at large, I never shall disown; and I shall always remember Elisa with pleasure, while I have a soul to animate these limbs. But to the point in debate I shall briefly speak"; and so forth, and so forth. The translator plods along, a sedulous ape; and one hardly knows whether most to lament the disruption of the poet's limbs, or to laugh at the incongruity of the whole thing— at Aeneas' debating society style, at the bad rhythms, the bad punctuation, the brackets for words *understood*, the jumble of you's and thou's.

Another example, also of grotesque character, may be

taken from the "only authorised translation" of Wagner's *Tristan and Isolde*, viz. the scene where the lovers meet just before their discovery by King Mark:—

> *Both*[2]. Art thou mine?
> Do I behold thee?
> Do I embrace thee?
> Can I believe it?
> At last! At last!
> Here on my breast!
> Do I then clasp thee?
> Is it thy own self?
> Are these thine eyes?
>
> . . . . .
> Endless pleasure!
> Boundless treasure!
> Ne'er to sever!
> Never! Never!

(2) We come next to writers who, suiting the canons of current taste, translate *pro bono publico* works that are valuable, but at the same time too outspoken for youthful readers or those of unformed judgment. Here questionable passages are obscured or omitted. Examples (from Greek, Latin, Arabian, Italian or other literatures) will quickly suggest themselves. One typical apologia, or statement of attitude, is given by Perrot d'Ablancourt in the preface to his French rendering of Lucian, of which the 4th edition was issued in 1664:

Les uns diront qu'il ne faloit pas traduire cet Auteur: les autres, qu'il le faloit traduire autrement. Je veus donc répondre à ces deux objections. . . . On ne peut nier que ce ne soit un des plus beaux Esprits de son siècle, qui a par tout de la mignardise et de l'agréëment, avec une humeur gaye et enjouée, et cette *urbanité Attique*, que nous appellerions en nôtre Langue une raillerie fine et delicate, sans parler de la néteté et de la pureté de son stile, jointes à son élegance et à sa politesse. Je le trouve seulement un peu grossier, dans les choses de l'Amour, soit que cela se doive imputer au genie de son tems, ou au sien. . . . Aussi jamais homme n'a mieux découvert la vanité et l'imposture des faux Dieux, ni l'orgueil et l'ignorance des Filosofes, avec la foiblesse et l'inconstan ce des choses humaines: et je doute qu'il y ait de meilleurs Livres pour ce regard. . . . On peut apprendre icy mile choses tres-curieuses, et c'est comme un bouquet de fleurs de ce qu'il y a de plus beau chez les Anciens. Je laisse à

---

[2] In the German, Isolde and Tristan speak these lines in alternation.

part, que les Fables y sont traîtées d'une façon ingenieuse, qui
est tres-propre à les faire retenir, et ne contribüe pas peu à
l'intelligence des Poëtes. Il ne faut donc pas trouver étrange
que je l'aye traduit. . . . et je suis d'autant moins blâmable,
que j'ay retranché ce qu'il y avait de plus sale, et adoucy en
quelques endroits, ce qui estoit trop libre, par où j'entre en la
justification de ma conduite, puisque voilà mon dessein assez
bien justifié par tant d'avantages qui peuvent revenir au public,
de la lecture de cet Auteur.[3]

(3) Examples of the more general class of broadly
serviceable translations, in which detailed adherence to
the text is not conspicuous, are everywhere obvious. Their
quality is again widely varied. Dryden's *Virgil* may be
cited for its literary merit and popular appeal.

(4) With regard to those on a more scholarly plane, which
read well in the new medium and indeed make excellent
literature, yet are not in all respects satisfactory to students,
one may instance some of Jowett's work (e.g. his version of
Thucydides). In such cases the wrestling with each difficulty is not always " to the fall "; the hold is at times slipped,
the crisis is evaded, and the translator continues the match
unruffled and imperturbable.

(5) As an example of the austere and exact form of
translation, which adheres rigidly to the text, one thinks
perhaps of work like Munro's *Lucretius*. If it exhibits a

---

[3] Lucien; de la traduction de N. Perrot, Sr. d'Ablancourt, 4th ed. J. de
Ravestein, Amsterdam, 1664.

[Some will say that this author should not have been translated; others
that he should have been translated differently. Let me answer these
two objections. . . . It cannot be denied that Lucian was one of the
brightest wits of his age: his fancy is always sprightly and entertaining,
his humour gay and lively. He has that Attic urbanity which we
Frenchmen might call an acute and delicate raillery. His style, too, has
precision and purity; it is elegant and polite. Still, I find him a little
coarse in matters of love: that may be due to the age he lived in, or to
himself. . . . No man has ever disclosed better the vanity and imposture
of the false gods, nor the pride and ignorance of the philosophers, nor the
feebleness and inconstancy of human affairs; and in this respect I doubt
if better books are to be found. From him one may learn a thousand
curious things, and his volume is like a bouquet of the fairest flowers of
antiquity. I pass by the fact that legends are there treated in such a
way as to fix them in the memory and to be not a little helpful for understanding the poets. It can hardly be thought strange, then, that I have
translated him . . . and I am the less worthy of blame in that I have
curtailed what is indecent and, in certain places, softened what is too
free. Thus my conduct is justified, whilst my design is sufficiently
vindicated by the many advantages which the public will gain from the
perusal of this author.]

certain harshness, yet its rugged veracity has notable merits
of its own.   In connection with such translation let me recall
the attitude, too, of Professor Phillimore, whose introduction
to his *Propertius* is extraordinarily interesting.   Part of
§V. may be quoted.   "A faithful translator is in duty bound
to be faithful in absurdity where, to the best of his appreciation, the Latin is absurd; he must not scruple at confusion
of metaphor or at outrageous hyperbole.   For example: if
Propertius wrote

tu patrui meritas conare anteire securis,

the translator must, to the best of his Latinity, weigh the
amount of metaphor which resides in *anteire*; and if he is
satisfied that the word is not a wholly defaced coin but
keeps its character, then he must render by *outstrip your
uncle's axes.*   And he ought to be moved by no such criticism
as 'This is impossible in English,' unless his critic can prove
that there is no such extravagance in the original, or at
least that the extravagance has been forced in the rendering.
Obeying the same rule he will reckon it a dishonesty to
palliate verbal brutalities, or to usurp the commentator's
office by unpicking the obscure accumulations of mythological allusion in which Propertius deals, or tacitly to amend
his defective economy of transitions.   Once play false to
this doctrine, and shirk the task of following out with the
humblest patience every nook and corner of the phrase, and
we stand in danger of lapsing into such unworkmanlike
flaccidity that Ovid in English will be undistinguishable from
Propertius, Homer appear faked into the semblance of
Apollonius Rhodius, and Plato and Thucydides read like
one and the same style."

Such was Professor Phillimore's fearless description of
what we may regard as the most rigid species of an austere
genus of translation—a species which I may perhaps call
the "photographic" species.   Little could be added to it,
unless it were Dean Plumptre's views concerning form, as
expressed in relation to his translation of Dante.   They are
given briefly in the publishers' preface to Vol I.[4] as follows:
"With regard to the *Terza Rima* of the 'Commedia' and the

[4] Dante, *The Divina Commedia and Canzoniere*, trans. by E. H.
Plumptre, 5 vols. Isbister & Co., London. 1899.

metrical forms of the 'Canzoniere,' the Dean was deeply
impressed with the conviction that, in default of absolute
identity of form, it is 'the duty and the wisdom of a translator to aim at the nearest possible analogue' attainable,
and to reproduce, as far as the nature of the English language
admits, the structure and recurrence of rhymes which give
sonnet and *canzone* their distinctive charm." If Professor
Phillimore could stomach an "uncle's axes" in English,
one might have expected him to insist not only on an elegiac
rendering of Propertius (uninfluenced by any debate whether
hexameters are tolerable or no in English), but also, as in
the Dean's own *tour de force* for Dante, on having an equal
number of lines in the original and the version. The late
Mr. John Payne, in his translation of Heine's *Last Poems*
went even further than this—and, as a review in the *Times
Literary Supplement* (Dec. 25, 1919) says, "failed disas-
trously." "The English line," he thought, "must be the
replica of the German, syllable for syllable, rhyme for rhyme,
double rhyme for double rhyme. The shifts to which he is
put in carrying out this scheme in our unsympathetic language often put a comic face upon a tragic couplet."

Such theorists may be regarded, then, as extremists in
this class of austere translators. Perhaps Dr. G. H. Rendall
may be more generally representative, and an extract from
his *Marcus Aurelius Antoninus to himself*[5] may serve as a
definite example of the type. It is from Book IX., § 28 *sq.*

Ταῦτα ἐστί τὰ τοῦ κόσμου
ἐγκύκλια, ἄνω κάτω, ἐξ αἰῶνος
εἰς αἰῶνα. καὶ ἤτοι ἐφ᾽ ἕκαστον
ὁρμᾷ ἡ τοῦ ὅλου διάνοια· ὅπερ
εἰ ἔστιν, ἀποδέχου τὸ ἐκείνης
ὁρμητόν· ἢ ἅπαξ ὥρμησε, τὰ
δὲ λοιπὰ κατ᾽ ἐπακολούθησιν
τινι. . . .

ἤδη πάντας ἡμᾶς γῆ καλύψει
ἔπειτα καὶ αὐτὴ μεταβαλεῖ.
κἀκεῖνα εἰς ἄπειρον μεταβαλεῖ
καὶ πάλιν ἐκεῖνα εἰς ἄπειρον
τὰς γὰρ ἐπικυματώσεις τῶν

Up and down, to and fro,
moves the world's round, from
age to age. Either the World-
mind imparts each individual
impulse—in which case accept
the impulse it imparts: or else it
gave the impulse once for all,
with all its long entail of consequence. . . .

Anon earth will cover us all;
then earth in its turn will change;
then the resultant of the change;
then the resultant of the resultant, and so *ad infinitum*. The

[5] Macmillan, 1899.

μεταβολῶν καὶ ἀλλοιώσεων
ἐνθυμούμενός τις, καὶ τὸ τάχος,
παντὸς θνητοῦ καταφρονήσει.
χειμάρρους ἡ τῶν ὅλων αἰτία·
πάντα φέρει. . . . .

Ἄνωθεν ἐπιθεωρεῖν ἀγέλας
μυρίας, καὶ τελετὰς μυρίας,
καὶ πλοῦν παντοῖον ἐν χειμῶσι
καὶ γαλήναις, καὶ διαφορὰς γινο-
μένων, συγγινομένων, ἀπογινο-
μένων. ἐπινόει δὲ καὶ τὸν ὑπ'
ἄλλων πάλαι βεβιωμένον βίον,
καὶ τὸν μετά σε βιωθησόμενον,
καὶ τὸν νῦν ἐν τοῖς βαρβάροις
ἔθνεσι βιούμενον· καὶ ὅσοι μὲν
οὐδὲ ὄνομά σου γινώσκουσιν,
ὅσοι δὲ τάχιστα ἐπιλήσονται,
ὅσοι δὲ ἐπαινοῦντες ἴσως νῦν σε
τάχιστα ψέξουσι· καὶ ὡς οὔτε
ἡ μνήμη ἀξιόλογόν γε οὔτε ἡ
δόξα, οὔτε ἄλλο τι τὸ σύμπαν.
Ἀταραξία μὲν περὶ τὰ ἀπὸ
τῆς ἐκτὸς αἰτίας συμβαίνοντα,
δικαιότης δὲ ἐν τοῖς παρὰ τὴν
ἐκ σοῦ αἰτίαν ἐνεργουμένοις·
τοῦτ' ἔστιν, ὁρμὴ καὶ πρᾶξις
καταλήγουσα ἐπ' αὐτὸ τὸ
κοινωνικῶς πρᾶξαι, ὡς τοῦτό
σοι κατὰ φύσιν ὄν.

billows of change and variation
roll apace, and he who ponders
them will feel contempt for all
things mortal. The universal
cause is like a winter torrent; it
sweeps all before it. . . .

. . . . . .

"*As from some eminence survey
the countless herds*" of men—
their thronging festivals, their
voyages of storm and voyages of
calm, the chequered phases of
their appearance, action, dis-
appearance; or imagine again the
life of ages past, the life of
generations to come, the life now
living among savage tribes; how
many have never heard your
name, how many will at once
forget it! how many who perhaps applaud you now, will very
soon revile! how valueless forsooth is memory, or fame, or all
else put together!

To vicissitudes caused from
without, be imperturbable: in
actions whose cause lies with
yourself, be just—in other words,
let impulse and act make social
action their one end, and so fulfil
the law of nature."

(6) By way of contrast, Meric Casaubon's version[6] of
part of the same passage may be given. It will illustrate
the Explanatory or Expansive Translation,[7] which as it
goes along amplifies and perhaps quaintly embellishes the
original, to some extent usurping, as Professor Phillimore
would say, "the commentator's office." The last two
paragraphs will suffice.

From some high place as it were to looke downe, and to behold
here flocks, and there sacrifices, without number; and all kinde

---

[6] *Marcus Aurelius Antoninus, his Meditations concerning himself*;
translated by M. Casaubon. (M. Flesher, London, 1634.)

[7] Amplification is also very noticeable in the Paraphrases and Parodies
(Nos. 9 and 10) mentioned below. But there the relation to the text is
obviously looser.

of navigation; some in a ruffe and stormie sea, and some in a
calme: the general differences, [or, *different estates*] of things,
some, that are now first upon being; the severall and mutuall
relations of those things that are together; and some other things
that are at their last.   Their lives also, who were long agoe,
and theirs who shall be hereafter, and the present estate and life
of those many nations of Barbares that are now in the world,
thou must likewise consider in thy minde.   And how many
there be, who never so much as heard of thy Name, how many
that will soone forget it; how many who but even now did
commend thee, within a very little while perchance, will speake
ill of thee.   So that neither fame, nor honour, nor anything else
that this world doth afford, is worth the while.   The summe
then of all; whatsoever doth happen unto thee, whereof God is
the cause, to accept it contentedly: whatsoever thou doest,
whereof thou thy selfe art the cause; to doe it justly: which will
be, if both in thy resolution, and in thy action thou have no
further end, then to doe good unto others, as being that, which
by thy naturall constitution, [or, *as a man;*] thou art bound unto.

The Greek of this passage contains 110 words, Rendall's
version 123, Casaubon's 240.

Of Casaubon's work perhaps one more example may be
given, for the sake of its current annotations and its picturesque charm.   It is from the beginning of Book V.:

In the morning when thou findest thy selfe unwilling to rise,
consider with thy selfe presently, it is to goe about a mans worke
that I am stirred up.   Am I then yet unwilling to goe about that,
for which I my selfe was borne and brought forth into this
world?   Or was I made for this, to lay me downe, and make
much of my selfe in a warme bed?   O but this is pleasing.
And was it then for this that wert borne, that thou mightest
enjoy pleasure?   Was it not in very truth for this, that thou
mightest [*alwayes*] be busie and in action?   Seest thou not
[*how all things in the world besides,*] how every tree and plant,
how sparrowes and ants, spiders and bees: how all in their kinde
are intent [*as it were*] *orderly* to performe whatsoever (towards
the preservation of this *orderly* Universe; or, *of this Universe,
which doth consist of order*) naturally doth become and belong
unto them?   And wilt not thou doe that, which belongs unto a
man to doe?   Wilt not thou runne to doe that, which thy nature
doth require?   But thou must have some rest.   Yes, thou must.
Nature hath of that also, as well as of eating and drinking,
allowed thee a certaine stint.   But thou goest beyond thy stint,
and beyond that which would suffice, and in matter of action
there thou comest short of that thou maist.   It must needs be
therefore, that thou dost not love thy selfe, for if thou didst,

thou wouldst also love thy Nature, and that which thy nature doth propose unto her self as her end.

In this passage Casaubon has three words for every two in Rendall, and two for every one in Marcus Aurelius. Casaubon lingers with delight over his work, and the austere brevity of the Emperor blossoms into the scholar's expansiveness.

As a lower species of this class, I spoke of the versions into which gratuitous flourishes and adjectives are inserted by the translator, to give "a more grateful taste." Viscount Preston, who turned into English Boethius' *Philosophiae Consolatio*,[8] may furnish an example: Book IV., Metrum IV., will serve.

> Quid tantos juvat excitare motus,
>   Et propria fatum sollicitare manu?
> Si mortem petitis, propinquet ipsa
>   Sponte sua, volucres nec remoratur equos.
> *Quos serpens leo tigris ursus apri*[9]
>   *Dente petunt, idem se tamen ense petunt.*
> An distant quia dissidentque mores,
>   Injustas acies et fera bella movent
> Alternisque volunt perire telis?
>   Non est justa satis saevitiae ratio.
> Vis aptam meritis vicem referre?
>   Dilige jure bonos et miseresce malis.

> Why should vain Man so great Commotions raise?
> Why with his Hand should he his Fate convey?
> If Death be sought, that comes, and never stays
> For winged Steeds to help it on its way,
> *They whom the Lion and the rugged Bear,*
> *The Indian Tiger, and the foaming Boar*
> *With eager Teeth, and with arm'd Claws do tear,*
> *Do stain their Swords in their own reeking Gore.*
> Is it because their Manners diff'ring are,
> And that their many Customs disagree,
> That they unjustly thus engage in War,
> And fiercely urge each others Destiny?
> This Reason is not just for shedding Blood.
> Wouldst thou to each Man give what he deserves;
> Love, as by Right thou art oblig'd, the Good,
> And pity him who from fair Vertue swerves.

[8] Boetius (A. M. S.), *Of the Consolation of Philosophy*, made English by Richard, Lord Viscount Preston. (Awnsham & Churchill, London, 1695.) P. 185. Preston explains his attitude in his Preface, p. xiii.-xiv.

[9] "Acri" is of course the better reading.

(7) We now come to the vivid translations, touched with genius, which in their new surroundings have a glowing life of their own: they are like scions grafted on an old and vigorous stock, which there thrive and blossom anew. As one example we shall think of the Authorised Version of the Bible, which has become "English of the English." On a briefer scale, there are some of the poems of H. A. J. Munro and of A. T. Barton. This class merges, at times almost insensibly, into two others: on the one hand into the Austere Class (5), as described above; on the other into the class of Adaptations, which follows next. In the Adaptations we shall see that allusions and images are freely changed to suit the traditions of the new language. In the present class, however, while such changes do occur, they are less frequent and less drastic, whether from a more careful handling of the material, or because originals have been chosen which contain ideas and images common to mankind in general. The resemblance to the Austere Class (5) will be apparent, to take a particular instance, in the following description of Munro's *Translations into Latin and Greek Verse*.[10] It is quoted from the Preface to that work written by Mr. J. D. Duff (of Cambridge).

Munro played the game according to the strictest rules. His verses are not a cento of tags from the Classics, dovetailed together with more or less ingenuity; he never admitted the conventional Latin which appears so often in modern Elegiacs. All that he found in the English had, of course, to re-appear in the Latin; still more, he did not like material re-casting of the form. The severity of his method leads at times to a certain baldness. But at other times, when he is inspired by his English and writing in a favourite metre—take as an instance the version in Glyconics of Deborah's Song—the result is something not easily forgotten and not easily distinguishable from an original work of art.

Munro's *Lucretius*, it will be remembered, was cited as one of the examples in Class (5). Let us take his Deborah's Song (from Judges v., verses 12, 24-31) to illustrate the present class.

Awake, awake, Deborah,	Suscitare, Dobura, te,
awake, awake, utter a song;	suscitare soporibus,
arise, Barak,	carmen edere tempus est;
and lead thy captivity captive,	surgat Abinoemides

---

[10] Published by E. Arnold, London, 1906.

thou son of Abinoam. . . .
Blessed above women
shall Jael the wife
of Heber the Kenite be,
blessed shall she be
above women in the tent.
He asked water,
and she gave him milk,
she brought forth butter
in a lordly dish.
She put her hand to the nail,
and her right hand to the
           workman's hammer,
and with the hammer she smote
           Sisera,
she smote off his head,
when she had pierced
and stricken through his temples.
At her feet he bowed,
he fell, he lay down:
at her feet he bowed, he fell:
where he bowed,
there he fell down dead.
The mother of Sisera
looked out at a window
and cried through the lattice
'why is his chariot so long in
           coming,
why tarry the wheels of his
           chariot?'
Her wise ladies answered her,
yea, she returned answer to
           herself
'Have they not sped?
have they not divided the spoil?
to every man a damsel or two?
to Sisera a prey of divers colours,
a prey of divers colours of
           needle-work,
of divers colours of needle-work
           on both sides,
meet for the necks
of them that take the spoil?'
So let all thine enemies
perish, o Lord:
but let them that love him
be as the sun,
when he goeth forth in his might.

ac domet domitorem.
Iam beatior omnibus,
contubernia quot tenent
omnia undique, feminis
Caeneos perhibebitur
Gellia uxor Heberi.
Illa, dux ubi simplicem
depoposcit aquam, dedit
lac et insuper obtulit
lactis, egregia gerens
in parapside, florem.
Clavum ibi arripuit manus
dextra malleolum fabri;
perforataque Sisarae

fissa tempora contudit,
discidit caput ictu.
Sidit, occidit ad pedes,
se posivit is: illius
sidit, occidit ad pedes,
quaque sidit, ibi ilico
procidit moribundus.

Sisareia ab aedibus
mater exseruit caput,
per fenestram ita clamitans
"cur morantur equi diu?

cur rotae retinentur?"

Tum catae comites, sibique
ipsa talia reddidit

"nonne res bene cesserit,
praeda contigerit, duae
cuique tresve puellae?
Praeda praeterea duci,
mille praeda coloribus,

picta vestis et hinc et hinc

utilis spoliantium
colla condecorare?"
Sic, Deus, pereat, tibi
quisquis invidiosus est;
quique te bene diligunt,
floreant, quasi vi sua
sol ut incipit ire.

As another example of this class the following version, by A. T. Barton, of Shakespeare's 12th Sonnet, will do admirably:

> When I do count the clock that tells the time,
> And see the brave day sunk in hideous night;
> When I behold the violet past prime,
> And sable curls all silver'd o'er with white;
> When lofty trees I see barren of leaves
> Which erst from heat did canopy the herd,
> And summer's green, all girded up in sheaves,
> Borne on the bier with white and bristly beard;
> Then of thy beauty do I question make,
> That thou among the wastes of time must go,
> Since sweets and beauties do themselves forsake
> And die as fast as they see others grow;
> 　And nothing 'gainst Time's scythe can make defence
> 　Save breed, to brave him when he takes thee hence.

> Si numero pulsus horae momenta notantes
> 　Seu video in nigra nocte perire diem;
> Purpura me violae marcescens sicubi movit
> 　Nigrave caesaries sparsa colore nivis;
> Si mihi celsa arbor foliis spoliata videtur
> 　Quae modo contra aestus texerat una gregem,
> Seu vehitur plaustro spicis in mergite vinctis
> 　Cana rigens, viruit quae modo verna seges;
> Tum mihi cura tua de forma multa recursat,
> 　Tu quod, ubi tempus cetera vastat, eas.
> Omnia namque solent formosa ac dulcia sese
> 　Linquere, dumque vident altera nata mori.
> Temporis et falcem fugiet res una, propago,
> 　Sospes, ubi victum te quoque tempus habet.

(8) In the next group—that of Adaptations—we have renderings in which the bonds of verbal correspondence often become relaxed in favour of a freer treatment. Ideas and allusions are now more often changed so as to fit an altered environment, or any special circumstances upon which the translator proposes to throw new light. We find in this class the work both of expert scholars and of less exact poets and men of letters.

That at times we need such changes of metaphors and allusions and names, etc., in turning one literature into another, is widely recognised: we thus escape anachronisms

and scholia, and secure instead what is living and familiar.
And if the point needed labouring it would be enough to
suggest that the forms of religion, the boundaries of geo-
graphy, the dominance of races, the achievements of arts
and sciences, the methods of government, all rise and fall
and change with the vicissitudes of the centuries. But enough
said: I am concerned with the actual practice of translators
rather than with its vindication.

As to examples, there is the *Rubâiyât of Omar Khayyâm* by
FitzGerald, whose adaptation of the more wordy Persian
poet exhibits that *laborem limae* which enhances the value
of the metal, adding more, as Pater puts it, than it takes
away.   Or one thinks, in another aspect, of Johnson's

> Let Observation, with extensive view,
> Survey mankind from China to Peru, *etc.*[11]

Again, one may recall Pope's *Imitations of Horace*; e.g.
Odes IV., 1:—

> Intermissa, Venus, diu
>   rursus bella moves? parce, precor, precor.
> Non sum qualis eram bonae
>   sub regno Cinarae.   Desine, dulcium
> mater saeva Cupidinum,
>   circa lustra decem flectere mollibus
> iam durum imperiis: abi
>   quo blandae iuvenum te revocant preces.   Etc.

> Again? new tumults in my breast?
>   Ah spare me, Venus! let me, let me rest!
> I am not now, alas! the man
>   As in the gentle reign of My Queen Anne.
> Ah sound no more thy soft alarms,
>   Nor circle sober fifty with thy Charms
> Mother too fierce of dear Desires!
>   Turn, turn to willing hearts your wanton fires.   Etc.

That other one of his, *Odes* IV., 9 (stanzas 1, 2, 3, 7),
which is still more drastic in its changes and which deserts
the Latin still more lightheartedly, may be better quoted
below among Paraphrases. But meanwhile two examples
may perhaps be given of Adaptations written by scholars
who keep closer to their originals. The first shall be a

---

[11] "Omnibus in terris, quae sunt a Gadibus usque Auroram et Gangen,"
etc.

Latin version,[12] of FitzGerald's *Omar Khayyâm*, by Mr. H. W. Greene, M.A. (Fellow of Magdalen). Stanzas XVI.–XVIII. will serve.

> The Worldly Hope men set their Hearts upon
> Turns Ashes—or it prospers; and anon,
>   Like Snow upon the Desert's dusty Face,
> Lighting a little hour or two—is gone.

> Think, in this battered Caravanserai
> Whose portals are alternate Night and Day,
>   How Sultan after Sultan with his Pomp
> Abode his destined Hour, and went his Way.

> They say the Lion and the Lizard keep
> The Courts where Jamshyd gloried and drank deep:
>   And Bahram, that great Hunter—the Wild Ass
> Stamps o'er his Head, but cannot break his Sleep.

> Quae terrena viris spes est ante omnia cordi
>   Fit cinis ante oculos, te capiente, tuos;
> Fac cepisse—brevi, ceu nix super arva renidet
>   Pulverulenta, micat, continuoque fugit.

> Cerne ruinosas quas incolis hospita sedes,
>   Queis sunt alternae noxque diesque fores.
> Has prius incoluit rex unus et alter, at olim
>   Jussi sunt propriam pergere quisque viam.

> Nunc quibus exultans quondam bibit Hector in aulis,
>   Inde leo latebras, inde lacerta, petit;
> Quo jacet Actaeon tumulum proculcat onagrus,
>   Non tamen est illi sic violanda quies.

My other illustration shall be a pretty Irish song by F. A. Fahy, which was happily turned into Latin elegiacs by Canon A. H. Cruickshank, D.Litt. (Professor of Greek and Classical Literature, Durham).[13]

> Oh! 'tis little Mary Cassidy's the cause of all my misery,
>   the raison that I am not now the boy I used to be;
> O she bates the beauties all that we read about in history,
>   sure half the country-side's as lost for her as me.
> Travel Ireland up and down, hill, village, vale, and town,
>   girl like my "cailin donn" you'll be looking for in vain:

[12] *Rubâiyât of Omar Khayyâm*, rendered into English verse by E. Fitzgerald, and into Latin by H. W. Greene. N. H. Dole, Boston, U.S.A., 1898.

[13] From *Fair Copies*. (Blackwell, Oxford, 1908.)

Oh! I'd rather live in poverty with little Mary Cassidy,
  than Emperor without her be, o'er Germany or Spain.
'Twas at the dance at Darmody's that first I caught a sight of
    her,
  and heard her sing an Irish song, till tears came in my eyes:
and ever since that blessed hour I'm dreaming day and night
    of her,
  the divil a wink of sleep I get from bed to rise.
Her cheek the rose of June, her song the lark in tune;
  working, resting, night or noon, she never laves my mind:
oh! till singing by my cabin-fire sits little Mary Cassidy,
  'tis little aise or happiness I'm sure I'll ever find.

Causa caputque mali nostri est formosa Neaera:
  hoc est cur non sim nunc ego qualis eram.
Illa quot historiis legimus supereminet omnes,
  magnaque pars iuvenum quo premor igne calet.
Lustraris patriam, nemora agros oppida pagos;
  omnes exsuperat flava puella comas.
Tecum habitare casam satius sit, parva Neaera,
  quam sine te Croesi condicione frui.
Hanc primum video Damone regente choreas;
  ad lacrimas moveor: carmina prisca canit.
Nocte dieque animum non cara relinquit imago,
  mane vigil noctu me vigilasse queror.
Ora colore rosam, numeros vox vincit alaudae:
  per requiem per opus cara figura placet.
Tum demum pacem carpemus et otia vera,
  cum sedet ad nostrum parva canitque focum.

As to other examples, are they not written in the *Antho-
logies*, the *Florilegia*, the *Serta*, the *Leptophylla*, the *Hortu-
lorum Flosculi*, the *Silviludia*, the *Arundines*, etc.—whence
one might glean a whole enchanting bookful?

(9) The Paraphrase was described as a freer kind of
Adaptation, professing no close adherence to the letter of
the original; it runs in a side-track approximately parallel.
Three examples will suffice. The first shall be Pope's
version of Horace (*Odes* IV., 9, stanzas 1, 2, 3, 7), which
was mentioned in the last class.

  Ne forte credas interitura, quae
  longe sonantem natus ad Aufidum
    non ante volgatas per artes
      verba loquor socianda chordis:

Non, si priores Maeonius tenet
sedes Homerus, Pindaricae latent
   Ceaeque et Alcaei minaces
     Stesichoraeque graves Camenae;
nec, si quid olim lusit Anacreon,
delevit aetas; spirat adhuc amor
   vivuntque commissi calores
     Aeoliae fidibus puellae . . .
Vixere fortes ante Agamemnona
multi; sed omnes illacrimabiles
   urgentur ignotique longa
     nocte, carent quia vate sacro.

Lest you should think that verse should die,
   Which sounds the Silver Thames along,
Taught, on the wings of Truth to fly
   Above the reach of vulgar song;

Tho' daring Milton sits sublime,
   In Spenser native Muses play;
Nor yet shall Waller yield to time,
   Nor pensive Cowley's moral lay.

Sages and Chiefs long since had birth
   Ere Cæsar was, or Newton nam'd;
These rais'd new Empires o'er the Earth,
   And those, new Heav'ns and Systems fram'd.

Vain was the Chief's, the Sage's pride!
They had no Poet, and they died.
In vain they schem'd, in vain they bled!
They had no Poet, and are dead.

The second shall be Milton's popular paraphrase of Psalm
136. Whether, as in nine other Psalms, he worked direct
from the original, or simply translated the prose of the
English into verse, is immaterial.

   Let us with a gladsome mind
   Praise the Lord, for he is kind,
     For his mercies aye endure,
     Ever faithful, ever sure. Etc.

For a third illustration, again from the Psalms, we may
turn to George Buchanan. He began his celebrated paraphrases in prison at Coimbra in Portugal, soon after the
authorisation of the Vulgate (in 1546) by the Council of

Trent. His versions, as is well known, have given delight to thousands, Psalm 104 in particular being appreciated. No. 137 may serve our purpose:

Dum procul a patria maesti Babylonis in oris
    Fluminis ad liquidas forte sedemus aquas,
Illa animum subiit species miseranda Sionis,
    Et nunquam patrii tecta videnda soli.
Flevimus, et gemitus luctantia verba repressit;
    Inque sinus liquidae decidit imber aquae.
Muta super virides pendebant nablia ramos,
    Et salices tacitas sustinuere lyras.
Ecce, ferox dominus, Solymae populator opimae,
    Exigit in mediis carmina laeta malis:
Qui patriam exilio nobis mutavit acerbo
    Nos jubet ad patrios verba referre modos,
Quale canebamus steterat dum celsa Sionis
    Regia, finitimis invidiosa locis.
Siccine divinos Babylon irrideat hymnos?
    Audiat et sanctos terra profana modos?
O Solymae, o adyta, et sacri penetralia templi,
    Ullane vos animo deleat hora meo?
Comprecor, ante meae capiant me oblivia dextrae,
    Nec memor argutae sit mea dextra lyrae:
Os mihi destituat vox, arescente palato,
    Haereat ad fauces aspera lingua meas:
Prima mihi vestrae nisi sint praeconia laudis:
    Hinc nisi laetitiae surgat origo meae.
At tu, quae nostrae insultavit laeta rapinae,
    Gentis Idumaeae, tu memor esto pater.
"Diripite, ex imis evertite fundamentis,
    Aequaque," clamabant, "reddite tecta solo."
Tu quoque crudeles, Babylon, dabis impia poenas,
    Et rerum instabiles experiere vices.
Felix qui nostris accedet cladibus ultor,
    Reddet ad exemplum qui tibi damnatum.
Felix qui tenero consperget saxa cerebro,
    Eripiens gremio pignora cara tuo.

It is perhaps worth noting that while the Authorised Version of the Psalm contains 164 words, Buchanan's paraphrase contains 211, in spite of the usually greater brevity of Latin.

(10) In Parody the style of the original is echoed with a genial, or a mocking, or a vulgar perversion. Burlesques, travesties, mock-heroics, are species of the genus. It is a

form of wit that perhaps flowers more freely and spontaneously, and is thought more worth while, amongst the
young and ebullient than amongst those who begin to
realise that

> "Old Time of late
> Has played the filibuster,"

and that their

> "Glass of fate
> Has shed another lustre."

Still, older *persifleurs* in this kind are not lacking.

Whether the parody is in the same tongue as the original,
or in another, the essence of the matter is this, that the
original is "translated" into a more or less distorted medium.
As for examples, there is the *Batrachomyomachia*; there are
Cotton's travesties of Virgil and Lucian; there is the work
of such men as the brothers Smith, J. Hookham Frere,
John Philips, Calverley, and many another.   J. K. Stephen's
well known sonnet, for instance, is refreshing:

> Two voices are there: one is of the deep;
> It learns the storm cloud's thunderous melody,
> Now roars, now murmurs with the changing sea,
> Now bird-like pipes, now closes soft in sleep:
> And one is of an old half-witted sheep
> Which bleats articulate monotony,
> And indicates that two and one are three,
> That grass is green, lakes damp, and mountains steep:
> And, Wordsworth, both are thine: at certain times
> Forth from the heart of thy melodious rhymes,
> The form and pressure of high thoughts will burst:
> At other times—good Lord! I'd rather be
> Quite unacquainted with the A.B.C.
> Than write such hopeless rubbish as thy worst.[14]

Reverting however to parody in a different language, a
few lines from Sir Owen Seaman's *Horace at Cambridge*[15]
(Of evergreen sirens: Quis multa gracilis?) may be quoted:

---

[14] Novi Lapsus, p. 106, in *Lapsus Calami*. Macmillan, Cambridge,
1905. It is worth remembering that a parodist has often a genuine admiration for the author whom he banters: witness this, again from Stephen
(*Parodist's Apology*, in *Lapsus Calami*):

> "If I've dared to laugh at you, Robert Browning,
> 'Tis with eyes that with you have often wept," etc.

A writer may put his victim on the hook "as if he loved him."

[15] Innes & Co., London, 1895.

Quis multa gracilis te puer in rosa
perfusus liquidis urget odoribus,
   grato, Pyrrha, sub antro?
     cui flavam religas comam,
simplex munditiis? . . .

What slender stripling in his primal year,
   His lip bedewed with "Tricholina,"
Amid your flower-pots with alluring leer
   Woos you, Georgina?

Across the counter leans his blazered arms,
   And, plying you with laboured sallies
Of amorous wit, around your waning charms
   Heavily dallies?

Who bids you bind your bun, I want to know,
   As once, my ever-verdant mignon,
For my sweet sake some thirty years ago
   You bound your chignon,

Simply mendacious in its artful dye,
   All golden as the daffodilly?   Etc.

(II)   In what I have called the Impressionistic rendering
we are, as in the translations first mentioned—No. I, the
dull, bald kind—again on the confines of our subject.   In
that first kind the text was sedulously adhered to, but the
spirit was, all too often, hopelessly lost.   Here the idea
alone remains—as a pretty changeling perhaps, or a witty
parody—while the text is abandoned.   Two examples may
be given, each summarising with epigrammatic brevity a
whole episode.   Crashaw's famous line describing the
turning of the water into wine at the marriage in Cana of
Galilee shall be the first:

     Nympha pudica deum vidit et erubuit.[16]

(Or, as some one had it, following Dryden's rendering
closely,
    "The conscious water saw its Lord, and blushed ").

---

[16] This is really the 4th line, though the essential one, of the whole verse,
which runs as follows:

   "Unde rubor vestris et non sua purpura lymphis?
    Quae rosa mirantes tam nova mutat aquas?
   Numen, convivae, praesens agnoscite Numen;
    Nympha pudica Deum vidit et erubuit.
               Sertum Carthusianum.

E

The other shall be furnished by Horace Walpole, who gaily interprets the Theseus and Ariadne incident thus:

> When Theseus from the fair he ruin'd fled,
> The nymph accepted Bacchus in his stead.
> The allegory, to my humble thinking,
> Means that deserted ladies take to drinking.[17]

II.

Let us now return to our original question, Why do men undertake such versions? The foregoing quotations, from texts and prefaces, will already have indicated that the motives are numerous. Translators, being artists in language, act like other artists: like actors who impersonate different characters; like musicians who are impelled to play particular instruments, or composers who adapt, let us say, folk-tunes or other themes to new conditions of musical composition; or like painters who take, for instance, old historical subjects and re-express them in the fashion of their own period and their own nationality. One is tempted to say, first of all and in a general sense, that men translate because "it is their nature." They do it because they are driven by inward impulse to this mode of self-expression. They do it because they enjoy doing it: enjoy it, that is, with the bitter-sweet joy that accompanies all intellectual or artistic effort. But secondly, and more specifically, a translator's thoughts may perhaps run, consciously or unconsciously, on some of the following lines. There may be the feeling that he has discovered good material which he desires to show to others; and he hopes thus to enrich the national literature. Should a version already exist, it is perhaps inaccurate, or antique and neglected; it could be bettered, made idiomatic of his time, and brought home to his contemporaries. Sometimes incidental suggestions may account for the undertaking of such work, as for instance when a lecturer or teacher, requiring a partial translation to illustrate a particular point, is led on to the idea of making

---

[17] *Horace Walpole.* (London, 1798.) Vol. IV. p. 404.

a complete version. Again, there may be the more personal feeling on the part of the translator that certain faculties need exercise: that his mind will be cleared, his outlook on things steadied, his perspective enlarged, and his general well-being promoted, by an engrossing occupation of this sort. So, in order to keep his weapons bright and to maintain keen and unimpaired an old skill in this or that literary form, he will employ particular metres or such and such prose styles, according as the original text strikes, for him, its answering note in the new tongue. Once more, there may be the wish to test his mastery, and to confirm his understanding, of some work whose beauty has profoundly affected him: he ponders it, and re-utters it as perfectly as he can, in a new harmony of alien words. The books translated may belong of course not to pure literature, but to science, or philosophy, or to religion, or what not; some further variety would then be introduced into the motives, though these would remain analogous to those mentioned. Love of laughter may be the lure, and the desire to have something light and amusing on hand to which a man can turn in spare hours or odd minutes. This aspect is illustrated in some of the parodies referred to, or in whimsies like that of Horace Walpole. It may be further illustrated in *jeux d'esprit* like these versions of nursery rhymes[18]:

Little Miss Muffet
Sat on a tuffet
  Eating her curds and whey;
There came a great spider
And sat down beside her,
  And frightened Miss Muffet
    away.

Muffa puellula
Sedit in herbula
  Acidum lac bibens;
Haud procul ab ea
Ingens aranea
  Terruit assidens!

Little Bo-peep
  Has lost her sheep
  And can't tell where to find them.
Let them alone,
And they'll come home
And bring their tails behind them.

Oves quas Bopippa pavit
Irrita desideravit,
  Quo abissent nesciens.

Mitte, parvula, ploratus:
Grex redibit, non vocatus,
  Caudas pone quatiens.

[18] By Professor J. Wight Duff, D.Litt., in *The Northerner: the Magazine of Armstrong College.*

To the same sort of motives may be attributed this rendering of *Jabberwocky* (from Alice *Through the Looking Glass*) into Latin elegiacs[19]:

> 'Twas brillig, and the slithy toves
>   Did gyre and gimble in the wabe;
> All mimsy were the borogoves,
>   And the mome raths outgrabe.
>
> "Beware the Jabberwock, my son!
>   The jaws that bite, the claws that catch!
> Beware the Jubjub bird, and shun
>   The frumious Bandersnatch!"
>
> He took his vorpal sword in hand:
>   Long time the manxome foe he sought—
> So rested he by the Tumtum tree,
>   And stood awhile in thought.
>
> And as in uffish thought he stood,
>   The Jabberwock, with eyes of flame,
> Came whiffling through the tulgey wood,
>   And burbled as it came.
>
> One, two! One, two! And through and through
>   The vorpal blade went snicker-snack!
> He left it dead, and with its head
>   He went galumphing back.
>
> "And hast thou slain the Jabberwock?
>   Come to my arms, my beamish boy!
> O frabjous day! Cullooh! Cullay!"
>   He chortled in his joy.

1.   Cesper erat; tunc lubriciles ultravia circum
>   Urgebant gyros gimbiculosque tophi;
> Maestenui visae borogovides ire meatu,
>   Et profugi gemitus exgrabuere rathae.

5.   "O fuge Iabrochium, sanguis meus! ille recurvis
>   Unguibus estque avidis dentibus ille minax:
> Ububae fuge cautus avis vim, grate, neque unquam
>   Foedarpax contra te frumiosus eat."

[19] Communicated to me years ago by Mr. T. A. Onions. It was done in Trinity College Lecture Room, May 3, 1879; but I have no note of the authorship. It has gaiety and ingenuity, and shows some liking for tags. He says that Mr. A. F. Chance, a master at his school, had it in a MS. book of translations; but whether it was written by Mr. Chance or by some one else, he does not know.

9. Vorpali gladio iuvenis succingitur; hostis
   Manxumus ad medium quaeritur usque diem:
   Iamque via fesso, sed plurima mente prementi,
   Tumtumiae frondis suaserat umbra moram.

13. Consilia interdum stetit egnia mente revolveus;
    At gravis in densa fronde susuffrus erat,
    Spiculaque ex oculis iacientis flammea tulscam
    Per silvam venit burbur Iabrochii.

17. Vorpali, semel atque iterum, collectus in ictum,
    Persnicuit gladio persnicuitque puer:
    Deinde galumphatus, spernens informe cadaver,
    Horrendum monstri rettulit ipse caput.

21. "Victor Iabrochii, spoliis insignis opimis
    Rursus in amplexus, O radiose, meos.
    O frabiosa dies! Callo clamateque calla."
    Vix potuit laetus chorticulare pater.

NOTES.—Line 1.   *Cesper*, from cena + vesper; *lubriciles*, from
                  lubricus + gracilis.   See the commentaries on
                  Humpty Dumpty's square, which will also
                  explain *ultravia* and *maestenui*.

„   5.   *Sanguis meus.*   Cf. Virgil *Aen.* VI., 836.

„   13.   *Egnia.*   Muffish = segnis; therefore uffish =
            egnis.

„   14.   *Susuffrus* is to whiffling as susurrus is to whist-
            ling.

„   15.   *Spicula.*   See the picture.

„   16.   *Burbur.*   Apparently a labial variation of
            murmur; stronger but more dissonant.

In a similar way, too, one might get a parody like
A. Sherman's *Homeric Games at an Ancient St. Andrews : an
Epyllium Edited from a Comparatively Modern Papyrus and
Shattered by means of the Higher Criticism.*[20]   In it modern
sports and undergraduate humours are "translated" into
Greek hexameters and into delightful English slang; there
is, moreover, the mock-solemn apparatus of prolegomena,
notes, and appendices on Goff or Gowf, Bridge, Smoking, etc.

To the great variety of motives for making translations
clues may at times obviously be got both from the forms in
which the versions are presented and from the introductions
by which they are accompanied.   The fact that a beautiful
form is in itself often the main lure may be illustrated by

[20] Published by James Thin, Edinburgh, 1911.

two examples. The first shall be from a contribution[21] to the quatercentenary number of *Alma Mater : the Aberdeen University Magazine*, 1906: "It has often crossed my mind," says the writer, "that in Latin there are many poems pre-eminently suited for translation into English sonnet-form. I have in view Latin poems which are short, and possess the semi-lyric quality of a good sonnet. Their cluster of thought and feeling makes a unity with some one note clearly dominant. Certain pieces of Catullus, Horace, Ovid, and later poets seem to produce on the mind something of the effect aimed at by the modern sonneteer. In these cases a successful translation is promised by one of the sonnet-forms which have become historic in English, rather than by imitation of the original meters. . . . With ideas of this sort in mind, I recently made a few experiments to illustrate my thesis." Four specimens follow: one from Catullus (*The Lament on Lesbia's Sparrow*), one from Horace (*To the Spring of Bandusia*), one from Petronius (*The Sleepless Lover*), and one from Statius (*To Sleep*). That from Catullus is as follows:

> Lugete, o Veneres Cupidinesque,
> Et quantumst hominum venustiorum.
> Passer mortuus est meae puellae,
> Passer, deliciae meae puellae,
> Quem plus illa oculis suis amabat.
> Nam mellitus erat, suamque norat
> Ipsam tam bene quam puella matrem;
> Nec sese a gremio illius movebat,
> Sed circumsiliens modo huc modo illuc
> Ad solam dominam usque pipilabat.
> Qui nunc it per iter tenebricosum
> Illuc unde negant redire quemquam.
> At vobis male sit, malae tenebrae,
> Orci quae omnia bella devoratis:
> Tam bellum mihi passerem abstulistis.
> Vae factum male! vae miselle passer!
> Tua nunc opera meae puellae
> Flendo turgiduli rubent ocelli.

Mourn all ye powers of Love and Loveliness!
Mourn all the world of taste for beauty rare!

[21] By Dr. J. Wight Duff, of Newcastle-upon-Tyne.

Dead is my lady's sparrow—to possess
　　Her pet was more than her own eyes to her.
The bird was honey-sweet, and knew its friend
　　As well as maiden knows a mother's face;
Nor left her lap, but twittered without end
　　To her alone, and hopped from place to place.
Now fares it on the darkling path of gloom
　　From which no traveller returns, 'tis said.
Hell-shades that prey on beauty, black your doom,
　　That carried my fair sparrow to the dead!
Woe, deed of ill! For thee, poor little bird,
　　My lady's eyes with tears are red and blurred.

For the second example, consider the following words, in which Dr. H. M. Butler[22] is speaking of the spell which certain literary forms can exercise:

While engaged on these poems, I was constantly haunted by the conviction that each Metre had, more or less, a personality of its own. It represented not so much an effort of ingenuity on the part of the translator as a self-assertion on the part of the metre itself. The metre in each case determined not the form only but the spirit. It not only expressed, it also created. Was this conviction wholly an illusion? I can imagine that even friendly critics might decide that it was this, and no more. But to myself it was a reality, almost a revelation.

On Dr. Butler's book the *Saturday Review* gives the following pretty comment: "His fine sense of style suggests to him

" 'That each bright metre, like a fairy elf,
Has subtle laws peculiar to itself,
Which gently guide th' half conscious poet's hand,
Suggest, persuade, less audibly command,
And choose, with silent but imperious claim,
Each word, each cadence, and each pastoral name.' "

Such a motive for translation, full as it is of the love of letters, may perhaps be reckoned among the most charming that one could desire. But Dr. Butler gives also further reasons. He has the quiet and modest expectation that "Children, Grandchildren, and intimate Friends may feel some interest,

[22] In a book of translations entitled *Some Leisure Hours of a Long Life.* (Bowes & Bowes, Cambridge, 1914.)

now and hereafter, in the thought or the memory that such innocent studies, however much open to the criticism of scholars, were at least unpretentious and perhaps characteristic." Elsewhere he speaks of a poetic appeal in his originals which was somewhat more general than the call of particular metres, and he explains the origin of three of his renderings thus. He says, "To the Greek translations," i.e. of certain passages from the Scriptures, "have been appended Latin Versions, more or less literal, of three of the most beautiful Collects. The attempt . . . helped me to feel, more than I had felt before, that the Collects are essentially poems." Of these versions one may be transcribed, partly because such treatment of the Collects is, I fancy, rare (though parts of the Bible have of course been turned into verse); and partly for the sake of its own beauty.

Almighty God, the Fountain of all wisdom, Who knowest our necessities before we ask, and our ignorance in asking; We beseech Thee to have compassion upon our infirmities; and those things which for our unworthiness we dare not, and for our blindness we cannot ask, vouchsafe to give us for the worthiness of Thy Son Jesus Christ our Lord.

> O sempiternae Fons sapientiae,
> Nondum inuocato numine praeuidens
> Quantis laboremus tenebris
> Rerum inopes, inopes precandi,
>
> Succurre egenis; quaeque uetat pudor
> Rogare, uel quae nox animi tegit,
> Largire, nec frustra petantur
> Immeritis benefacta Christi.

From Dr. Butler, finally, can be shown more explicitly how motives of piety may produce translations; for, in summing up, with a sweet dignity and charm, his way of regarding his translations and occasional verses, he tells us that throughout a period of nearly seventy years, during all the experiences and shifting scenes traversed from his schooldays onwards, "the old habit of making verses . . . has clung to me as a faithful companion, helping me, however imperfectly, to keep in touch with the thoughts of the wise, the pious, and the pure, and giving a kind of quiet unity to a

life of some labours and many distractions." Of the aged
scholar's long and devout art one other brief example may
be given:

> Lord, it is not life to live
> If Thy presence Thou deny;
> Lord, if Thou Thy presence give,
> 'Tis no longer death to die.

> Σοῦ μὲν παρόντος, οὐκέτ' ἔστι κατθανεῖν,
> ἐπεὶ θανόντες ζῶμεν εἰ δὲ μὴ πάρει,
> καὶ ζῶντες οὐχὶ ζῶμεν, ἀλλ' ἐσμὲν νεκροί.

III.

Is translation, as many people seem to think, a merely
imitative and mechanical art? Or can it under certain
conditions claim, like other arts, the title of original work?
The answer depends, I think, in the first place, on how the
work is done; that is to say, on the kinds of translation
to which we refer. Summing up what has gone before,
perhaps we might say that a translation tends to become
an original work in proportion as it attains, in its new
medium, independent vitality. The essential thing is that
the new work should be able to stand alone; stand intelligibly, in its own artistic fitness or beauty; and that it should
be desired and read for its own sake, even by those who
know nothing of the material on which primarily it is based.
If readers do know the original, their interest will of course
be enhanced, and their pleasure increased. To attain this
independence translators must have thoroughly digested and
assimilated their subject, and they must have the creative
ability to re-express it in their own terms and their own way.
It must be their own offspring, deliberately matured, and
having inevitably an infusion of their own personality.
In this sense the Authorised Version of the Bible will seem
to be an original English work, and one not due to a merely
copying craftsmanship in which "this word" is turned into
"that word." To many people too Butcher and Lang's
Odyssey will have similar claims; or FitzGerald's *Omar
Khayyâm*; or, as we have seen, some of Munro's Latin
versions. Many other examples might be given; among
them, perhaps, even Pope's *Homer*. ("A very pretty poem,

Mr. Pope; only you must not call it Homer": which criticism at least shows that its value and vitality were its own, and independent of the Greek.)

Our answer to the question depends also on what we understand generally by the word translation, and on what we mean by originality in other arts. Hitherto we have used the word translation mainly in the restricted sense of expressing in English, say, or Latin or Greek, something which was at first written in another language. But this is only one particular case of the more general sense of translation, viz. the expressing in a new form things or ideas which already existed in another form. This general sense is of course widely recognised, but an instance or two may be given. The actor's art offers a good illustration. The words which he is to employ are set down for him. These words he has to interpret into the language of movement and gesture, of voice, of facial expression: in a word, he must translate them into visible and audible human emotion; he must impersonate the characters. The impersonations which different actors present are as varied in kind and value as are the literary translations referred to earlier. There is vulgar ranting, full of misapprehensions; there is passable characterisation; there is parody, or burlesque; there is explanatory acting (with asides to the audience, such as Shakespeare laughingly gives us in *Pyramus and Thisbe*); there is exposition which delights discerning critics by its genius of insight. As to the last, Lamb's essay *On Some of the old Actors* leaps to the mind. Take this description of Bensley, for instance:

His voice had the dissonance, and at times the inspiriting effect, of the trumpet. His gait was uncouth and stiff, but no way embarrassed by affectation. . . . He seized the moment of passion with greatest truth; like a faithful clock, never striking before the time; never anticipating or leading you to anticipate. He was totally destitute of trick or artifice. He seemed come upon the stage to do the poet's message simply, and he did it with as genuine fidelity as the nuncios in Homer deliver the errands of the gods. He let the passion or the sentiment do its own work without prop or bolstering. He would have scorned to mountebank it; and betrayed none of that CLEVERNESS which is the bane of serious acting.

This description of Bensley's acting recalls in certain respects Professor Phillimore's doctrine of translation. It forms too a very interesting parallel to the description, already quoted, of the art of H. A. J. Munro, in which the result is said to be something not readily forgotten and not easily distinguishable from an original work of art. In Bensley as in Munro, there is the occasional harshness of diction, the scrupulous fidelity to the text, the eschewing of "gag" and "tag," and the vivid sincerity of the whole presentment. At the greater moments their results, gained in each case by sheer honesty, penetrating insight, and complete technical skill, were living creations.

The case of the musical artist, who in his performance translates into the language of sound the silent work of composers, is also analogous. We have a similar range in varieties and values. There is the plodding "dull dog"; there is the mountebank of music, with his gratuitous flourishes and twiddles; there is the commentator with his audible asides; and there are the great, simple artists, through whose renderings "deep calleth unto deep."

In the composition itself of music, translation also plays its part. Religious emotions, the sounds and aspects of nature, various forms of human gaiety or grief are expressed in a new language, viz. that of musical sounds. Moreover, music of previous composers is by editors or fresh composers arranged, and popularised, and adapted to fresh conditions times out of number.

Poets and prose-writers again, in their descriptions of nature, exhibit suggestive parallels to the literary translator and his art: what they see and hear they must convert into a new medium—that of words. So too with pictorial artists. Thomas Bewick, for instance, to take a local illustration, translated riverside scenes, and incidents of the rural Human Comedy, into the language of draughtsmanship and of exquisite wood-engraving. Caricaturists also, like the parodists and persifleurs described above, echo the form of their originals with laughter and mocking perversion.

It would be interesting, indeed, to work out the thesis that all literary and artistic and scientific utterance is a translation of one group of conceptions into another group, of one mode of thought into another mode. The result may be a "poor" translation, worse than the original; or it may be a photographic translation, in which *this thing* corresponds duly to *that thing*; or it may be a "transcendent" translation, in which the original is lifted on to a higher and more universal plane. If the thesis were established, the question how far translation (in the ordinary linguistic sense) is imitative,·and how far it is original, would be merged into the general question how far any literary or artistic or scientific work is merely imitative, how far original. Be that as it may, however, perhaps enough has been said to suggest that at least to the greater translators, as to the greater exponents in dramatic, in musical and in other arts, the claim and title of originality should not be denied.

The art of translation, then, or—as it seems fundamentally to be—of expressing existing ideas in new forms, has a big range of possibilities. At its worst it may be bald, ugly, grotesque; at its best it may be full of suggestion, vigour and loveliness. Translation holds up the mirror to her votaries, and they reveal themselves after their kind, some good, some bad. Her spell and her fascination are upon many men: upon the 'prentice hand (like piper grating on his "wretched straw"), and upon the master of the craft; on the literary hack, and on the thoughtful and brilliant scholar.

To furnish a "dying fall" to these inquiries—these observations of an amateur—two final examples may be given. The first shall be a version (of Psalm 42) quoted in Kennard's *Arundines Sturi*.[23] It is by Arthur Johnston; and the late Professor Robinson Ellis, in his copy of the book (now in my possession), had noted it as "good."

1. As the hart panteth after the water brooks, so panteth my soul after thee, O God.
2. My soul thirsteth for God, for the living God: when shall I come and appear before God?
3. My tears have been my meat day and night, while they continually say unto me, Where is thy God?
4. When I remember these things, I pour out my soul in me: for I had gone with the multitude, I went with them to the house of God, with the voice of joy and praise, with a multitude that kept holyday.

[23] Ed. by R. B. Kennard. (J. Parker, Oxford, 1878.) P. 13

5. Why art thou cast down, O my soul? and why art thou disquieted in me? hope thou in God: for I shall yet praise him for the help of his countenance.

6. O my God, my soul is cast down within me: therefore will I remember thee from the land of Jordan, and of the Hermonites, from the hill Mizar.

7. Deep calleth unto deep at the noise of thy waterspouts; all thy waves and thy billows are gone over me.

8. Yet the Lord will command his lovingkindness in the day time, and in the night his song shall be with me, and my prayer unto the God of my life.

9. I will say unto God my rock, Why hast thou forgotten me? why go I mourning because of the oppression of the enemy?

10. As with a sword in my bones, mine enemies reproach me; while they say daily unto me, Where is thy God?

11. Why art thou cast down, O my soul? and why art thou disquieted within me? hope thou in God; for I shall yet praise him, who is the health of my countenance, and my God.

Cervus ut, in medio celsis de montibus aestu
    Actus, in algentes fertur anhelus aquas;
Sic mea vitali satiari Numinis unda
    Mens avet, et Domini languet amore sui:
Gestit et optat amans, vitae se adjungere fonti:
    His mihi deliciis quae dabit hora frui?
Dum sine fine petunt—ubi sit Deus iste timendus?—
    Sunt misero lachrymae nocte dieque dapes.
Scandere me quoties memini penetralia sacra,
    Et longo populos ordine pone sequi;
Aurea dum recolo missas ad sidera voces,
    Et plausum festis quem decet esse choris;
In lachrymas totus miser et suspiria solvor,
    Inter et aerumnas est mihi dulce queri.
Cur ita turbaris? cur te, Mens, dejicis exspes?
    Cur ita me torques anxia? fide Deo:
Scilicet hic placido recreat mihi lumine pectus;
    Et mihi materies unica laudis erit.
Dum queror, in mentem, liquidis Jordanis ab undis,
    Sepositisque jugis, Tu mihi saepe redis.
Gurgitis est gurges, rauci comes aequoris aequor:
    Fluctibus infelix obruor usque novis.
Luce, sed in media bonitas tua fulsit abysso:
    Nocte, Parens vitae, tu mihi carmen eris.
Tunc ego, cur, dicam, capiunt Te oblivia nostri?
    Rerum Opifex, animae portus et aura meae!
Cur prope confectum curis, lachrymisque sepultum,
    Me sinis immani durus ab hoste premi?

Hic petit insultans, ubi sis?—ego vulneror inde,
　Ensis et in morem permeat ossa dolor.
Cur ita turbaris? Cur te, Mens, dejicis exspes?
　Cur ita me torques anxia? Fide Deo.
Scilicet Hic placido recreat mihi lumine pectus,
　Et mihi materies unica laudis erit.

For the last example we will return to our starting point,
viz., A. T. Barton's translation of Shakespeare's Sonnets.
In No. 99 the flowers are arraigned for wearing beauties
stolen from the lover: and because Translation is another
"sweet thief" such as they, we will take this sonnet.

The forward violet thus did I chide:
Sweet thief, whence didst thou steal thy sweet that smells,
If not from my love's breath? The purple pride
Which on thy soft cheek for complexion dwells
In my love's veins thou hast too grossly dyed.
The lily I condemned for thy hand,
And buds of marjoram hath stol'n thy hair;
The roses fearfully on thorns did stand,
One blushing shame, another white despair;
A third, nor red nor white, had stol'n of both
And to his robbery had annex'd thy breath;
But, for his theft, in pride of all his growth
A vengeful canker eat him up to death.
　More flowers I noted, yet I none could see
　But sweet or colour it had stol'n from thee.

Increpito veris violam "fur dulcis, odorem
　Unde nisi ex dominae surripis ore meae?
Haec tibi sublucens tam molli purpura voltu
　Heu male virgineo sanguine tincta rubet."
Lilia de furto damnat tua palma, tuumque
　Crinem in amaracina suspicor esse coma.
Stat rosa quaeque tremens in spinis, conscia culpae,
　Huic pudor erubuit, palluit illa metu.
Tertia rubra albet binos furata colores,
　Ac furtis animam iunxerat illa tuam.
Quod sceleris propter media florente iuventa
　Illa rosa ultrici peste subesa perit.
Plus etiam vidi florum, nec in omnibus unum
　Cui tua non species aut tuus esset odor.

If, in following the lure of translation, men answer her
call by "golden strands of song" like these, they are, by
the charm they add to life, already justified of their pursuit:
their "cocoon-spinning" is vindicated.

A Gourmand's Breviary

AN entertaining little book, expounding the art of your true gourmand—that fine art which enables him to make great and prolonged meals without subsequent penalties—fell into my hands a good many years ago. I dipped into it casually now and again, not without chuckling amusement; but it is only in these last few days, when away on a holiday, that I have read it more attentively. The irony of these war times and the regulations of our Food Controller have between them furnished the *sauce piquante* required to bring out its full flavour.

The book in question was published in 1805 (An. XIII.), and is the second revised edition of the second issue of the *Almanach des Gourmands, servant de guide dans les moyens de faire excellente chère. Par un vieil amateur.* Its size is 6 by 3½ inches, and it contains 318 pages. The frontispiece is a copper plate (Grimod de la Reyniere inv., Dunant del., Mariage sc.) representing *Les Audiences d'un Gourmand.* The Gourmand is seated in his reception room at a table furnished with pens, ink and paper. From the ceiling hangs game of various kinds (deer, hare, boar), and the shelves are crowded with birds, pasties, jars of olive oil, &c., and some books on the alimentary art. His visitors troop in bearing their "credentials," viz. a great pasty and other delicacies. The Gourmand takes careful note of these credentials (*légitimations*) which, when they have been carefully tested by an impartial jury and himself, will have judgment pronounced upon them. The best of them will receive honourable mention in the *Almanach des Gourmands*, whilst the artists who devised them may hope to be ranked as experts. The editor promises that he will not regret the indigestions such examinations may cause him if only the culinary art of Paris is thereby encouraged and enriched.

This second year's issue is dedicated to M. Camerani, a manager of the *Opéra Comique National,* and his claims to the distinction are stated in the Dedicatory Epistle. In the first place he was the inventor of the *potage* n amed after him, and had communicated the recipe to the editor for publication. It is given on pp. 30–32, and among its ingredients were the finest Neapolitan macaroni and Parmesan cheese, butter from Gournai or Isigny (according to the season), about two dozen livers of fat chickens, celery, and many other vegetables. Camerani often regaled his friends with this *potage.* It had a delicious taste, and was the cause of many indigestions. Secondly, he had introduced into Paris some wonderful *langues de bœuf à la vénitienne.* Thirdly, he had the recipe for the best macaronis, which he often prepared for his friends with his own hands, with the result that they could never enjoy any others. Both his erudition and his practical skill in the culinary art were admirable, and his *Potage,* his *Langues,* and his *Macaronis* entitled him to the first rank among artists: his immortality was secure.

But he had other qualifications. As our author says, addressing him: "Need we speak of your taste, with its perfect appreciation of the most exquisite viands? of the sensitiveness of your palate, with its skill and delicacy in judging the rarest wines? of the greatness of your appetite, which gives a festive welcome to all the dishes of the most sumptuous table? or, lastly, of that recuperating slumber into which you fall about the middle of the second service of courses,[1] and which gives you the means of doing honour to the third, since it restores you, in a sense, to a state of fasting? . . . Such are briefly, sir, the rare and sublime qualities by which you have deserved our gratitude and our humble veneration. But appetite, taste, and erudition of this kind are still not enough to characterise a true gourmand. These virtues are only valid during a repast, whereas it is at all hours of the day that one should be able to pick out the man who is truly worthy of that venerable name—a name which so many of the uninitiated usurp,

---

[1] The numerous dishes or courses were apparently grouped in three services, though there would be four on ceremonial occasions.

or vainly strive to merit, though they win nothing from their
efforts save quite ignoble indigestions. . . . The gourmand
is not only he who eats mightily, discriminatingly, re-
flectively, sensually; who leaves nothing on his plate or in
his glass; who has never distressed his Amphitryon by a
refusal, nor his neighbour by an access of abstemiousness:
he must join to the most assertive appetite that jovial
humour without which the richest banquet is but a melan-
choly hecatomb: ever prompt at repartee, he must have all
the senses with which nature has endowed him in a state of
continual activity: lastly, his memory must be enriched with
a crowd of anecdotes, stories, and amusing tales which he
judiciously 'places' in the intervals of the courses and in
the interstices of the viands, so that abstemious folk may
pardon his appetite."

After the preliminary pages the author gets to business.
He discusses first the *coup d'avant* or *apéritif*—a large
glass of vermouth, absinthe, rum, or *eau-de-vie*, taken
before the meal to promote appetite. He is not disposed
to commend it, at least for French stomachs; Russians and
Germans may stand it.   Then he speaks of the *coup d'après*,
or half-glass of pure wine taken immediately after the soup.
Here the case is different, and Parisians regard it as so
beneficial that, as their proverb goes, the *coup d'après*
docks a fee from the doctor. Next he treats of the soup,
which is to a dinner what the portico or peristyle is to a
building; that is to say, not only is it the first item, but it
should be so composed as to give a true idea of the feast,
pretty much as the overture of a comic opera should an-
nounce the subject of the work.

The chapter that follows describes the functions and
qualifications of the best host, the true Amphitryon.   There
is, for a rich man, no finer rôle to play in this bad, sad world
than that of Amphitryon. Money alone, however, is not
enough. One man spends much, but gives poor fare;
another, with only a moderate fortune, gives excellent dinners.
The calling of an Amphitryon, like all others, requires a
noviciate, a varied training. It offers many difficulties.
To fill the part well, one must join to a good education a
profound knowledge both of men and of good cheer. Our

F

Amphitryon must have an extremely delicate palate, and
must take infinite pains in the choice of foods and of wines.
Among wines, for instance, there is so much knavish adul-
teration that nine-tenths of the tables in Paris are ill supplied
with them.   If one wants natural wines of good quality,
one should get hold of them as they leave the vat, in the
same way as a man used to secure a young girl on her leaving
the convent school if he wanted to be tolerably sure of having
a spotless bride.   Nor are the moral qualities less necessary
than those others in a perfect host.   How can he gather
amiable guests and place them judiciously if he does not
possess a happy tact, a great skill in men, and a knowledge
of the world?   One cannot eat for five hours without a break,
however excellent the dinner; and man, being a feeble and
impotent creature, soon finds, alas! limits to his appetite.
The most intrepid eater becomes sated when he has gone
steadily through the first two series of courses; and that
is the time when one feels the need of having an amiable
neighbour, and of being able to converse with him.   But
too often the guests do not know each other; and if the host,
who should know them all, has not taken the trouble to
place them suitably, they will find themselves reciprocally
paralysed.[2]

Guests, on their side, should do all they can to praise, and
encourage, and facilitate the efforts of their host, and should
pay their scot in merry *bons mots*, witty repartees, and short
and amusing tales.   The shorter the tales the better.
As Madame Geoffrin once told a young provincial, "il faut se
munir de grands couteaux et de petites histoires."—"You
should be furnished with long knives and short stories."

Déjeuner is treated next.   Since the Revolution, the
dinner hour had been postponed to 6.0 o'clock, and something more substantial than a cup of tea, or *eau de tilleul*
(lime-flower tisane, perhaps), or *café-au-lait*, was needed to
bridge the interval.   Hence the idle rich supported nature
on a mighty meal in which ten sorts of cold meats figured,
with flagons of different wines; or possibly there might be
hot dishes, such as *membres de volaille en papillotes de*

---

[2] To this subject our author reverts on p. 154, in a chapter headed
Du Voisinage à Table.

Madame Hardy, poulets à la tartare, or at least *petits patés au jus de M. Ronget,* kidneys, and small sausages. In this preliminary repast the *pièces de résistance* were *salades de volaille* and game pasties, preceded in winter time almost invariably by oysters from the famous *Rocher de Cancale.* But such fare was ill suited to persons of moderate means, or to the modest foster-child of the Muses; and our author commends in its place a light and nutritive chocolate such as M. de Bauve prepared. Other sorts were too often deleterious concoctions, containing anything but the genuine cacao. But on de Bauve's article delicate people would thrive, and ladies in particular would look in their mirrors with gratification. They would contemplate with delight their rosy tints and the freshness of their sweet and blooming skin; and perhaps would feel a sentiment of gratitude towards the author of this little work: "O utinam!"—he exclaims.

Now we get a eulogy of the dinner. Dining, he says, is always the most interesting action of the day, and one performs it with the utmost zeal, pleasure and appetite. A coquette would renounce her power of pleasing, a poet his expectation of praise, a Gascon his claim to prompt credence, a comedian his applause, and a rich Midas his incense of flattery, sooner than Parisians (seven-eighths of them, at least) would forego the making of a good meal. That no author has hitherto treated dining with the full gravity it deserves, and written philosophically about it, has ever seemed surprising. How many things might be said about this memorable action which is renewed 365 times a year! Our friend describes the gloom of the guests if dinner is by some accident delayed; their relief when it is announced and they can hurry to their places; their growing satisfaction; their exhilaration as course follows course, and the wine circulates; their joyous chat and *bons mots*; their half-confidences and declarations. It is mostly the ladies and the children who enjoy the sweets, for your true diner rarely wants anything after the roast; what he eats beyond that he takes out of compliment to the host. As to the dessert which follows, that will appeal more to the sight than to the other senses of the gourmand. He will indeed be gratified by its brilliancy and its *éclat*: it is to the dinner what the *gironde* is to a display of fireworks. To produce a good dessert a man needs a combination of many artistic talents; he also needs much money, since a dessert alone has at times cost 10,000 crowns. Yet the true and faithful gastronomer is content to admire; and he prizes an appropriate morsel of cheese far more than all these pompous and brilliant decorations. Such, says our author, is a brief *aperçu* of a dinner—that pleasure which one may renew thirty times a month.

The *Goûter* had fallen into neglect. It was an afternoon collation, which, though it now lingered only in the provinces (where it still made its appeal to ladies and children), had at one time been popular among the *élite* of Paris. Its appropriate setting was a rustic scene. "What more delicious," says our author, "than a *goûter champêtre* taken in the shade of a green, laughing grove, under the azure vault of a sky that is pure and serene, or under a bower of vines whose golden, appetising clusters hang down right on to the table of this joyous feast! Such a repast is not only one for children: all lovers of Nature can appreciate its charm. A careless gaiety animates all its scenes, whilst for a timid and modest beauty, sitting at these charming love-feasts near her lord, the sentiment of tender passion relishes the sweeter that it is eagerly shared." Our author's vignette is quite *à la Watteau*. But in his own day, he goes on, men had grown sombre and disillusioned. Yet for the sake of the curious he gives a full account of the suitable viands; and he refers those who want to realise what the true *goûter* was to a description of one given in *La Nouvelle Héloïse*.

Suppers, in the good old days before the Revolution, were more particularly the festivals of Love and Literary Wit (*Amour et Apollon*). They now linger only in the memory of those who were so fortunate as to live before the great tragedy. "In those joyous days everyone was genuinely French, that is, was amiable, and gifted with the grace, tact, and lightness which belong truly to this happy nation alone. It is the one nation that understands pleasure, and especially the pleasure of conversation, seeing that it alone

can lightly, and with an indescribable charm, gather the
bloom from any subject, pressing nowhere too heavily:
it is the bee that sucks all flowers though lingering in none.
Other races of Europe discourse and argue: the Frenchman
alone knows how to converse. Where are now those
delightful suppers to which Court, Town and Letters brought
of their best and friendliest; those gatherings in the sanc-
tuaries of opulence in which there reigned, far more than in
the Republic which succeeded them, that Equality without
which all pleasures are void ; those gatherings in which rank,
birth, wit, and fortune displayed themselves only in a contest
of amenity, taste, and elegance; in which there was no
proud superiority, because knowledge of the world had
taught men to be considerate of the *amour-propre* of others;
in which the reigning beauty, the poet in fashion, the
minister in power, and the courtier in favour appeared
indiscriminately under the banners of true liberty? Alas!
they have disappeared in that revolutionary torrent which
has invaded and ravaged all. We have seen them replaced
by those Fraternal repasts which were held at the edge of
the street gutters, repasts in which there reigned that
brotherhood of Cain and Abel ostentatiously placarded over
all our buildings. Never have there been less Liberty and
Equality in France than during the time when every house
bore their ensign upon its walls." The author presently
turns to the gastronomic point of view, and gives briefly
what he calls the *composition nutritive* of a correct supper.

The Dessert, as has been said, should be the brilliant part
of a festivity, and its appearance should surprise, delight,
and enchant the guests. Its main function is to gratify
the mind and the sight, other senses having been already
appeased. The art of producing a good dessert was of
late growth among the French, who owed it, like all other
arts, to Italy. French caterers formerly relied on an
immense profusion and a ponderous elegance; taste and
delicacy were lacking. An idea of what was then in vogue
may be got from the picture of the Wedding of Cana, by
Paul Veronese. But the art developed. The serving of
natural and preserved fruits led to the happy idea of representing the trees on which the fruits grew. Delightful

imitations of fruit-groves were designed; then movement
and grace were given by covering the table with trays of
varnished metal, which the artist decorated with mirrors.
With sand of different colours he represented flowers, and
added the charm and variety of *parterres*: while the illusion
was completed by providing these *parterres* with little men
and women of sugar, correctly coloured.   Thus one beheld
a choice and elegant company walking on a smooth lawn
enamelled with flowers.   This sort of design first appeared
in 1725, at the marriage of Louis XV. and Marie de Pologne.
But arts link themselves with other arts, and rise to their
zenith ere they decline.   Desforges came, the father of the
author of *La Femme Jalouse* and *Tom Jones à Londres*.
He it was who introduced imitation grass.   Then Dutfoy
called architecture to the aid of decoration.   To the orchards,
lawns, and *parterres* of his predecessors he added palaces,
in which all the orders were represented; and their severe
proportions, perfect taste, and great size attest the man of
genius.   He fashioned for us temples surmounted by a vast
dome or an elegant cupola, and adorned with a great
peristyle, with galleries that grew dim in the distance, and
with beautiful porticoes.   Columns, entablatures, capitals,
pediments, architraves, cornices, &c.—all were constructed
in accordance with the rules of the art.   The profiles were
of remarkable purity, and the ornaments in excellent taste.
Elegant groves and bushes, so accurately done as to produce
the most perfect illusion, made up the landscape of these
palaces and temples, and there were richly composed groups
of figures in *biscuit de Sèvres*.   All was movement and life,
and the skilful play of lights gave a touch of magical beauty
to the spectacle.   Then a change came over the scene: a
slow match, carefully hidden, had been lighted, and suddenly
the temple was over-arched with fragrant fire of every colour,
whilst a thousand firespouts leapt up to the ceiling.   The
guests were under a canopy of flaming sparks, and eyes and
nostrils alike were deliciously gratified.   The sparks, too,
though so brilliant, were quite innocuous, and no harm
came even to the most delicate materials.   A scene of
fairyland such as M. Dutfoy could produce made a perfect
termination to a sumptuous repast.   Our author mentions

other schemes of decoration, and the various edibles appropriate to this course. People talked of such desserts for six months, and the glory which the Amphitryon achieved repaid him for all the trouble he had taken.

The various meals having been now described, our author passes to other matters. He greatly dislikes the presence of servants throughout a meal: their eyes devour all the meats greedily, their ears suck up the conversation, and their tongues are ever ready to slander or denounce their masters, how kind soever these masters had been during twenty or thirty years, This has been proved constantly and terribly, during the Revolution. By a suitable arrangement, however, of the dishes and the wine the trouble can be avoided. All that is necessary is that at each group of courses (*service*) a few should enter and clear the table, and spread it afresh under the eye of the *maître d'hôtel*. The guests will then feel freer in their talk; though even so politics should, for other reasons, be avoided. Subjects that are gayer, and more "digestive," should be chosen—such as literature, plays, gallantry, love, and the art of alimentation: these are inexhaustible sources of joyous discussion. Scandal and backbiting should be eschewed: only ill-conditioned persons talk scandal at table, for nothing should make people more indulgent than good cheer and hilarity.

Then comes a chapter on "Mustard and *Sirops* considered philosophically." Without mustard, he says, certain meats are as dull as a pointless epigram (*ne sont qu'une épigramme sans sel*). The function of *sirops* is to maintain serenity of mind, sweetness of character, and tranquillity of brain.

Under the heading "A new and easy means of securing appetite," he discusses the waters of Montlignon, near Montmorency. "Not far from Montmorency, at the bottom of that charming valley so famous for its cherries, for its delightful temperature, and for the long stay made in it by J. J. Rousseau, in an enchanting site equally adorned by Art and Nature, there is a nymph who takes Gourmands under her protection, and offers them at all hours her generous help. A wondrous water flows unceasingly from her beneficent urn, and this water gives, to whosoever drinks it, the means of making daily five or six meals and of braving indigestions, nay, of never getting them, since it communicates to the gastric juices of the weakest stomach an indomitable vigour."

Another section of the book is headed "Variétés Nutritives." It contains various maxims, reflections, and anecdotes, as well as some general principles of politeness and good cheer extracted from the famous rules (not published) of M. Aze:—

A gourmand, for instance, who is worthy of the name, takes his soup and his coffee scalding hot.

A good host abhors a vacuum (to wit, in his guests' plates and glasses).

The greatest annoyance you can cause a gourmand is to interrupt him in the exercise of his jaws (*mâchoires*): never call on people when they are eating.

Guests should never arrive when dinner has begun: those who do so should refrain from entering, even if they have to go fasting the rest of the day, as a punishment for their unpunctuality.

It is far easier to dance a minuet well than to carve certain joints.

One of M. Aze's rules, which were in force in more than one society of Paris, provided that a fine of 500 francs, or £20, should be paid by anyone who had accepted an invitation to dinner and failed to come. The fine was reduced to 300 francs, or £12, if he had given two full days' notice of his inability to be there.

Five hours at table is reasonable when there are many courses and abundant cheer.

Everything has its price in this deplorable world—especially a good dinner. If, then, a guest cannot pay for it in kind, he must discharge the debt in another fashion. The most common is to bring one's tongue in evidence instead of one's purse, and to amuse the company if one is unable to regale it. That is what is called paying in monkey's money (*monnaie de singe*); but the coin is current in Paris.

The "call" after dinner (*la visite de digestion*) is a sacred duty which no one who understands life, and who has not lost the appetite for another opportunity, fails to discharge. The length of this visit is determined, in some countries, by the generosity of the repast of which one thus acknowledges receipt. Some calls have been known to last three hours. Many Amphitryons would excuse such and such guests from so lengthy a mark of gratitude.

When one has dined with a man, one should abstain from speaking ill of him for a period varying from eight days to

six months, according to the excellence of the entertainment.
But the Amphitryon can always bind the guest again by a
fresh invitation. One must admit that, of all ways of stopping
scandal concerning oneself, this is not the least amiable.

There was a celebrated gourmand who maintained that
the pleasures procurable from choice viands far outlast
those to be got from the company of even the most beautiful
women. Can you compare any woman, he said, with those
wonderful partridges of Cahors, Languedoc, and the
Cevennes, whose divine fragrance surpasses all the perfumes
of Arabia? Could you set them beside those *patés*, made
from the livers of geese or ducks, to which the towns of
Strasburg, Toulouse, and Auch owe the best part of their
fame? No: the jubilant faces of all sons of Comus are a
sufficient witness, when contrasted with the faces, so pale
and wan, of those who are sick with love.

In the chapter already referred to on "One's neighbours
at table," there is an anecdote of two dinners given to the
same group of twenty-five guests, one of whom relates his
experience. They were complete strangers to one another,
though that difficulty might have been got over if the seating
had been judicious. Unfortunately, however, there was
no sort of arrangement. A *curé* found himself between a
poet and a comedian; a tradesman sat beside a judge;
soldiers beside bankers; artists beside merchants; and so
on. The poet wanted to discuss his tragedy, which had
fallen flat, with the *curé*, who was full of the success of his
own last sermon; nor could the *curé*, on the other side, understand a word of the tales of the *coulisses* with which the
comedian sought to regale him. An author began a gram-
matical discussion with a merchant, who only replied with
laments over the stagnation of the sugar and coffee markets.
Interests were all at variance, and the neighbours spoke,
as it were, in different tongues. Silence and gloom soon
fell upon them all. Afterwards, when the narrator went to
pay his *visite de digestion*, his host lamented the ill-success
of the evening. His visitor explained politely how he
thought the trouble might have been avoided, and suggested
that it would have been better if the poet had been placed
beside the comedian, who would have sympathised with him

and consoled him for his bad luck, and have entertained him with a picture of the inner life of his theatre. The *curé* and the magistrate, who were grave and sensible men, would have done well together. The bankers and the merchants would have talked a common language and would have enlightened one another concerning the Bourse and commerce, and the profits they had made. The host was pleased with the idea, and soon after issued another invitation to the same guests. He arranged them as his friend had suggested, and the dinner was an admirable success.

The "Song of a Gourmand" is presently given. It is an imitation of a drinking-song by Maître Adam of Nevers, and recalls to one's mind the old students' song

> Mihi est propositum
> In taberna mori.

The last verse may be roughly translated as follows:—

> Fain were I could Death's stroke fall
> In some rapture of repast!
> Be the table-cloth my pall,
> Lay me 'mid four dishes vast.
> For my epitaph I'd prize
> This—if brief 'tis still the best:
> "Here the first of poets lies
> "Dead, through failing to digest."[3]

We are next given a dissertation and eulogy upon pastry, which is to cooking what the figures of rhetoric are to a speech. Women and children especially delight in it, though no dinner is at all complete without it. To make it well is a fine art and a costly. The sumptuous Teas, which had now largely replaced the old-time suppers, needed the finest, lightest, and most brilliant *pâtisseries* to augment their splendour, and to help the consumption of punch, tea, liqueurs, and wine. The mere pastry eaten at such meals might well cost 300 francs.

[3] Je veux que la mort me frappe
Au milieu d'un grand repas :
Qu'on m'enterre sous la nappe
Entre quatre larges plats,
Et que sur ma tombe on mette
Cette courte inscription:
"Ci-gît le premier Poète,
"Mort d'une indigestion."

The chapter on Wine is not among the least entertaining.
It begins with the aphorism of a *Procureur d'une Abbaye
de Chanoines Reguliers*, that "there is too much wine in the
world for saying mass: there is not enough for turning mills:
therefore we must drink it." This, says our author, is a
veritable apophthegm: the more you consider it, the more
you realise that it is a "réflexion profonde et lumineuse."
"Wine is," he goes on in a rhapsody, "according to many
authors, the best friend of man when used in moderation,
and his worst foe when taken in excess. It is the companion of our life, the consoler of our chagrins, the ornament
of our prosperity, the chief source of our real sensations.
It is the milk of old men, the balm of the adult, and the
vehicle of gourmands.[4] The best repast without wine is
like a ball without its orchestra, a comedian without his
rouge, or a chemist without his quinine." The true gourmand knows that its effects, to a man who eats his fill, are
far less unchancy than to the seeming-abstemious man
who toys with his food. The gourmand will not fear any
generous, natural wine, however potent; and, given equal
heads, will always outdo the mere drinker, who does not
eat, by four bottles." As Dominie Sampson would say:
"Pro-di-gi-ous!"

The gourmand's philosophy is expounded as follows:
"As regards pleasure, it is only the present that counts;
the past too often offers only regrets, the future only fears.
Life is so short that we must neither look too far back, nor
too far forward, if we would enjoy it. Let us know how to
fix our happiness in our glass and our plate; and, trusting
ourselves to divine Providence, which never abandoned its
children to want, let us do honour to to-day's dinner, without
thought of to-morrow's. For one man who dies of hunger
a thousand die of indigestion: what an eternal argument
to a gourmand is this, for confidence, and even for hope."
The fitting end to our "happy warrior" is clearly a heroic
indigestion.

Our author, continuing his discourse on wines, laments
that a good cellar is now as rare in Paris as a good poem.
He presently passes to beer, with its colours, qualities, and

---

[4] *I.e.* apparently, it carries their food down smoothly.

cellaring methods; and to cider, which is sadly adulterated in Paris. As to liqueurs, which are the best? He leaves the task of answering this difficult question to more erudite gourmands than himself:

Non nostrum inter vos tantas componere lites.

Anon comes a chapter on coffee. *Café à l'eau* is the thing, not *café au lait*, which is most unwholesome. Its colour should be blond rather than brown, and certainly not black. To it, when rightly prepared (and this is seldom done), we owe *l'inappréciable bonheur de pouvoir manger longtemps et beaucoup sans être incommodé*. Coffee is "the inspirer of men of letters, the digestive of gourmands, and the nectar of all men."

The maintenance of the cook's health is a most important matter. It must be scrupulously and tenderly watched. His calling is in many ways unwholesome, and even dangerous. There are the continual smells and vapours, the glare of the fire, the smoke, the heat, the need of frequent drinking (generally of bad wine), &c., &c. A primary condition of his engagement should be that he is to take the medicine deemed needful by his employer without grumbling. If he begins seasoning his dishes too highly, it is a sure sign that he needs doctoring. That is the only way to maintain the delicacy of his palate, which otherwise becomes "as dull as a judge's conscience."

A chapter on cheese follows; then one on the killing of birds, game, &c., by electrocution—a method recently discovered by Dr. Franklin. This method at once renders the meat as tender as if it had been long hung, and secures promptly the right degree of mortification.

The inventor of sweets (*confitures*) is unknown. "What a pity! He deserves a statue of sugar-candy, and we would suck our lips every time we pronounced his name."

The great art of Gastronomy and Alimentation involves nearly every kind of human knowledge. Physical science, useful arts, chemistry, painting, sculpture, architecture, geometry, pyrotechnics—all are needed to equip the perfect artist. The inventions of the Genius of Good Cheer should be promptly recorded in some *Journal Gourmand*, along with all celebrated indigestions. Some such discoveries are given, e.g. that of a delicious *ramequin de Bourgogne*, which led, it is true, to several indigestions, but the process by which they were got was so delightful that "no one even thought of complaining."

There is a short note on the kind of songs suitable for the table, and those of Pannard, Collé, Piron, Laittaignant and others are commended as being at once decorous and gay. Songs should never begin before the end of the dessert: they often continue until the dawn.

The last chapter of the book is upon—Indigestions. Hints for avoiding them or treating them are given. The final paragraph is as follows: "By taking these precautions one will be able to eat much, and eat for a long time, without being incommoded; and that is what a gourmand must desire above everything. An illness which puts one on diet for several days is for him, more than for any other, a really vexatious matter: it is so much cut off his life. And what a life that of a true Gourmand is! It is an earthly counterpart of the Paradise of Mahomet."

August, 1917.

A Newcastle Seaman 100 Years Ago

In 1827 a Newcastle printer, R. T. Edgar, of Pilgrim Street, issued a book called *A Narrative of the Adventures of a Greenwich Pensioner, Written by Himself*. The title-page does not reveal the author's name, though it is clear that his initials were G. W. from the signature to the introduction.

Who was G. W.? It is not till p. 194 that we incidentally find the answer to the question. On that page a list is given of the killed or wounded in an engagement fought in 1812 off the mouth of the river Po. Among the names is George Watson, able seaman, and the narrative makes it plain that this is the man with whom we are concerned. He was a Novocastrian, and his book, which is now I believe quite rare, is interesting for a good many reasons. For one thing, it gives a picture of the sort of life led by seamen in the Napoleonic wars. For another, it describes the state of things in various ports at which the ships touched. It affords too an insight into the *régime* of naval hospitals 100 years ago, and reveals the quality of the nurses who were employed there. From the more personal point of view, we get Watson's opinion concerning his shipmates and superior officers. Last, but not least, we have the character of the man himself portrayed. In his short life as a seaman— he was only 20 when disabled—he was observant, honest and courageous; in his cups he was at times unruly; if, along with his shipmates, he was now and again wild in other ways, such faults were transitory, and he recognised them as faults: indeed, considering the company he was obliged to keep, the wonder is that he was not a great deal worse. We take leave of him at the last as a man who had resolved to live in a straight and modest manner, who had taken to reading, had learnt to enjoy certain poets, and had himself written two works. One of these, probably not printed, was a poem on the battle in which he was disabled; and

the other was the prose *Narrative* with which we are now
concerned.

I propose to give some account of his life up to the time
when he became a Greenwich pensioner; for that is as far
as the book carries us.

George Watson was born in Newcastle in September,
1792. His father was a mariner, and was often from home,
so that his mother had to look after the growing family as
best she could. George stayed at school till he was $9\frac{1}{2}$,
and left at the conclusion of the peace of Amiens.[1] His
education therefore was of the slightest. His father, who
had returned from a man-of-war, consented to take him on
his next voyage. Some time after Christmas they started
in a collier for London. The ship was leaky, pumps were
going day and night, and it blew a gale all the way to
Yarmouth roads; so the boy, who was sea-sick, had a bad
time. They reached Blackwall, and anchored astern of a
frigate. At midnight a boat's crew from the frigate came
on board to impress men for the King's ship, since war had
again been declared with France.[2] George's father, and
every one else except the master and three youngsters, were
carried off. The collier was badly moored; the wind rose,
the cable parted, and there were no sailors to set things
right. She drifted away, fortunately clearing other vessels,
and got stranded on a mud bank. In the morning they were
got off by some men from the shore, and they reached
London. Meanwhile the father got discharged from the
tender, but fearing to be taken again went to Greenland, and
George returned to Newcastle. After a time his mother
agreed to have him bound apprentice as a sailor on a large
ship in the Baltic trade. From that time until the writing
of the book in 1826, George saw his father only twice (in
1803 at Dantzig, in 1804 at Quebec), and heard of him once
(in 1811). Of his mother's lasting influence for good he
speaks several times; and the recollection of her "pious
vigilance" whilst he was a child remained with him.

By the time he was 12, he was, as he says, "becoming a
sailor quite fast." He could "reef, steer, heave the lead,

---

[1] 27 March, 1802.
[2] War was not actually declared till May, 1803.

furl a sail, splice a rope, and so forth," and things were going pretty well with him. Trouble came, however. In Canada two of the sailors wrongfully accused him of stealing some money, and a vindictive Newcastle man, the carpenter, gave support to the charge. The boy protested his innocence hotly and with tears, but could not prove it. The men obtained leave three times from the foolish mate, who had been left in charge, to go on shore in order, as they said, to consult a witch upon the matter; actually they had a carouse. The money was afterwards conveniently "found," but the taunts about thieving continued, and the lad in his bitter resentment broke his apprenticeship, ran off, and got on board the Osborne, which was lying two miles higher up the St. Lawrence, and was short of hands. After they had sailed he was taken to the captain, who received him kindly, and engaged him at £3 a month; and the lad soon won the approval of officers and men. The Osborne was accompanying, as stern commodore, a fleet of 30 merchantmen, under convoy of the frigate Champion. Watson soon had his experience of a battle at sea; for a French man-of-war, commanded by one of Napoleon's brothers, attacked the fleet, and only seven or eight of the ships escaped. The frigate and troop-ships got away safely, as the French preferred to attack, plunder and burn the unarmed vessels, and did not pursue the rest. The Osborne had sixteen 18-pounders, and 500 soldiers on board. Watson says that had there been two English frigates instead of one, they would not have run from the French man-of-war. They reached Portsmouth two months after leaving Quebec. The voyage being concluded, Watson was again engaged on the Osborne, which was next to go on a secret expedition, carrying troops, to Rio de la Plata and Buenos Ayres. Meanwhile they stayed in Portsmouth for a fortnight to refit, and Watson speaks of the numerous docks and building ways, the impregnable fortifications, and the chain to draw across the entrance of the port and keep out the enemy's ships. Joining the fleet at Spithead they started for South America, being 50 sail in all, and having about 10,000 men on board.

The incidents of the voyage are described in considerable

detail: the fish they caught (which made a welcome change
in their mess), the storms of rain, thunder and lightning,
the rough sports and ceremonies when crossing the equator.
After three months their provisions were running short,
so they made for Rio de Janeiro.   Here the change of food
was very welcome, and, as Watson says, "every one seemed
to enjoy the benefits of the refreshments they received,
and the repose of a snug anchorage, secure from the noise of
the tempest and the lash of the unruly wave, so sweet is
rest to the weary soul, or a good port after a long and tedious
voyage." Watson was interested in the abundant fruits
(pineapples, apricots, peaches, bananas, yams, sweet potatoes,
etc.), in the gaily coloured birds, and in the negro slaves
who worked there. A tragic incident occurred, and it
appalled him. A new maintop gallant mast was being
hoisted up when the rope broke. The mast fell on deck
from its great height, horribly crushing to death "a lovely
boy about 5 years old" who was just stretching out his hand
to his mother for a piece of bread she had offered him.
"The hapless woman fell at the feet of her darling," whilst
the little baby she was nursing tumbled from her knees
and rolled in its brother's blood.

The fleet was ready in about a fortnight and went on to
La Plata. At Maldonado the troops on each ship were
reviewed by Generals Achmuty[3] and Lumley, who arranged
for the landing at Monte Video. Then came the disem-
barkation, the fighting as they approached the town (which
was ten miles away), the siege, and the final storming on
3rd February, 1807. The carnage on both sides was very
heavy. Watson gives a picturesque description of the
whole episode. He partly observed things from his ship
through a spy-glass, partly shared in them. Here they
stayed more than six months. The Spaniards Watson
did not admire; for he says "they were as lazy as other
Spaniards, lousey, superstitious, and lascivious, and con-
sequently cowardly—there is nothing so likely to enervate
the mind as a licentious and immoral course of conduct."
They seemed to be honest, however. The women
were pretty but very dark; they were of "a grave and

---

[3] *I.e.* Sir Samuel Auchmuty.

apparently contemplative countenance, but for all that very volatile and gay, which is the natural effect of a warm climate." Provisions were cheap. A horse and saddle could be bought for five dollars, a bullock for 5s. Watson describes, too, the town and its defences. His recollections may or may not have been accurate, but for a lad of 14 or 15 he seems to have noticed things carefully. He tells a tale of a wounded officer who had previously treated his men with the harshest contempt and insults: "When any of them came near him on board of ship, he would exclaim 'get off you beast, you stink!' Now, when he sought their help, they retaliated by telling him to 'lie there and stink; or who stinks now?'" Watson thinks this barbarous, even to an enemy—but after all not unnatural. He moralises thus: "Contempt engenders hatred in the most peaceful and refined bosoms, much more must it do so in those who are accustomed to the roughest scenes of bloodshed and war."

The British overran the neighbourhood for some miles, and after receiving a strong reinforcement from England, under General Whitlock,[4] advanced with about 15,000 men against Buenos Ayres. The attack was apparently badly planned, and, in spite of brave fighting, ended in ignominious defeat. As a result, the whole district, including Monte Video, had to be promptly evacuated; as Watson says, "a fair wind soon carried us out of sight of the country we had come so far, to win so hardly, and loose so foolishly, and, in a few days, we found ourselves on the Ocean again." [This was in July, 1807.]

After crossing the equator they encountered several gales, and got the rigging somewhat damaged. A little later there was a serious risk; a brandy cask caught fire and "exploded like gunpowder: this was directly under the magazine wherein were 300 barrels of ball cartridges." The mate, who was in the hold trimming the ship, "fled immediately, and getting out, cried 'the ship is on fire!' that was enough! the report had been heard from under the powder room, and everybody on deck expected every moment to see her blow up! all ran forward to escape the explosion; the sick, and wounded scarcely able to move, attempted to get on

---

[4] *I.e.* John Whitelock.

deck, some wanting arms, and others legs, and having got out of bed they could not support themselves, and by falling on the deck many of them were brought to a sudden and unexpected death, for we had to throw fourteen of them overboard before we reached Portsmouth. The uproar on the ship was awful, and the scene distressing in the utmost degree; here you might see mothers binding their children to them, ready to jump overboard, and shun the schorching [*sic*] flame, their [there] wives and husbands embracing as for the last time, the picture of despair, and almost every countenance bearing marks of consternation and woe, while the cries of the women and children were calculated to awaken all the sympathies of our nature, and fill the heart with anguish and doleful bitterness." However, the peril was averted in time. "One of the young men in the hold, seeing the mate run away and the flames arising right under the magazine, hasted at his peril, and took a blanket, that was near, and wet it in the pickle of a pork cask, and threw it over the burning spirits, then drew near and smothered out the flame; he got his face, hair, and arms, sorely singed and scorched by it, and when he was helped on deck, to get the air, one of the military officers approached and struck him, supposing it was his neglect that had caused all the disorder we had witnessed, whereas he providentially was the means of saving more than three hundred lives—

> Thus Justice while she winks at crimes,
> Stumbles on innocence sometimes.—*Hudibras*."

Watson has descriptive powers; and the extracts given will serve to reveal both the qualities and the defects of his style.

About three weeks later the fleet got scattered by a gale. The Osborne (Watson's ship) sprang a leak, and the pumps were kept going day and night till England was reached (Dec. 1807). She anchored off Cowes, but had another adventure; for during some careless (perhaps too convivial) watch her cable parted and she drifted six miles through a lot of other ships, and went ashore off Stoke. Next day they got her off and went to Portsmouth, where the rest of the army had arrived and been landed some time before. The Captain (Marmaduke Howlett), though intending to discharge most of the crew, wanted Watson to remain with him, and was ready to take him to his home in Hull, to board him, put him to school, make a man of him, and to promote him when he was fit. Watson however declined this generous kindness. He had chummed up with a worthless Newcastle man given to drink and other vices, who was one of those to be discharged, and he had resolved to share fortunes with him. So he got his wages and went off. In riper years he remembered with remorse his disrespect and his neglected opportunities. In the midst of their swaggering and tippling and capering, he got a letter from his mother, urging him to come home. He read it with tears behind a boat. His friend was willing to go north, but the masters of certain Sunderland brigs refused to take them, fearing they had run away from a man-of-war; and they had not money for the coach. They joined the Scipio, a transport bound for Gibraltar, Watson getting, through Captain Howlett's recommendation, an increase in wages. A month's money, which he got in advance, he sent to his mother. They left Spithead with a fleet of 60 sail. In the Bay, on Christmas Day, 1807, they encountered a hurricane. Five soldiers were washed overboard; three were drowned, but the other two, strangely enough, were tossed by the waves back on board as the ship rolled. It was the worst sea Watson ever saw. They managed to get to Falmouth, where they found most of the other vessels, and lay there six weeks refitting. They then sailed again and reached Gibraltar after a delightful run of about eight days. They disembarked the troops and washed and repaired the vessel. Watson's companion, after being reprimanded for drunkenness, ran off and joined the Fame (a 74). Watson describes Gibraltar, and narrates two adventures he had there. In the first he and a shipmate had supped with certain others at an inn, and the charge had been exorbitant, leaving them but little money. These two, when the rest had gone to bed, were left by the host drunk on the floor in a locked room. By midnight they slept themselves sober, and to avoid paying another heavy charge for breakfast and lodging they resolved to escape. They squeezed themselves through a large wooden pane above the door, tumbled headlong, at the risk of breaking their necks, on to the platform of a fort behind the hotel, and so evaded their rapacious host. In the second adventure, he was with the ship's cook, a black man who fancied himself as a lady-killer, and who got himself up gaily, parting his "wooly foretop" and dressing it in two tufts which he turned back under his beaver. After strolling about they found themselves outside a church when the matin bell was ringing. They stood for a little, and then the cook, attracted by the folk, proposed that they should go in. They did so, and found themselves beside a bevy of damsels "apparently absorbed in heavenly meditation." Watson behaved decorously and knelt down. When the cook removed his hat however his "much admired plaits of wool unconsciously rose erect, on each side of his forehead, like horns." The girls promptly noticed them and shrieked out that he was the devil, and fled to the protection of a priest who was at hand. The place got into an uproar, and order was only restored when the guard was called in and the cook and Watson were marched off to the guard house. The priest made a formal charge against them as enemies to religion and God, accusing the cook especially of "coming into the church in character of the 'Arch Fiend' to disturb the devotions of the congregation and drive the ladies from their prayers." Watson was told he could go, but he would not desert his comrade. Ultimately the officer of the guard, who thought the whole affair ridiculous, dismissed them both, advising them to keep clear of such weak, superstitious people.

Watson did not rejoin the Scipio. After parting from the cook he went to the Fame to see his Newcastle crony, and once there he resolved to stay with him, abandoning his own ship. This, as he says, was the beginning of his martial career, "the portal to many hair breath [sic] escapes 'by flood and field'."

Watson was presently made coxswain to one of the Fame's large boats. He won the approbation both of the Captain (R. H. A. Bennet) and the 1st Lieutenant (Mr. Norton). The Captain was considerate of his men, looking after their comfort, and not overdriving them; he tried, too, to make them all expert in every branch of ship-board life, and in the use of guns, broadswords, cutlasses, etc. They first went to Cadiz to join the fleet blockading the French and Spaniards there, and remained hanging about until Spain declared war against France. The French ships were then attacked and captured by the Spanish. Next the English ships joined the Toulon fleet under Lord Collingwood. Six months later they went to the Gulf of Rosas to succour the Spanish garrison; and here Watson came for the first time under the immediate fire of the foe. They had a lively time, but found the Spanish troops, sent from the garrison to help them, rather a sorry support. In spite of reinforcement by the Magnificent and the Imperious (the latter commanded by Lord Cochrane), they had presently to abandon the enterprise: so they blew up the fort and left only its ruins to the French. Making their way to Mahon in Minorca, they lay there a month or more, refitting. This town they often saw whilst attached to the Toulon fleet, for nearly the whole squadron wintered there for two or three months at a time. Watson liked the place—perhaps because he fell in love with a young damsel there called Maria. He was attracted by her gentleness and sweetness; for his mind, he tells us, "was never congenial to that harsh, unmannered roughness, which characterises the general addresses of seamen, and which is the very reverse of feminine softness and sociability. Moreover, being of a contemplative disposition, what could I behold to fix my admiration on so much as women? they are the fairest and dearest, and the kindest of the visible creation, and though everything in nature is calculated to excite our wonder, and inspire us with love to Him that made the whole, yet chiefly so is woman! man's dearer self!"

When the ship was in good trim they rejoined the fleet at Toulon, where Watson had a narrow escape from death. He was up aloft, busy with the fore topsail, about 4 feet below the yard, when on some sudden danger of collision with another ship the lieutenant ordered the sail to be "shivered" so as to cause the Fame to drop astern. "The topsail shook," he says, "and I was hanging by it with nothing to support me: it blew pretty fresh and every moment threatened to shake me off. I was first thrown one way, and then another, till I gave up every hope of life, I caught hold of some of the points by which the sail is reefed, that were nearest to me, and twisted them round my wrist, and kept my hold till the skin was torn, my shins also were chaffed [*sic*] much at the same time, the sailors both in the top and on the deck, when they saw my situation told the Lieutenant, that he might fill the sail, he said he could not, owing to the posture of the two ships, and concluded by saying, 'what is the fool doing there?' so much for the pity of that worthy personage; by this time I was nearly exhausted, my shipmates advised me to throw myself clear of the ship, into the sea, as my only resource for safety, for if I fell by the fluttering of the sail, I might fall on deck and be instantly killed; I came to the resolution recommended, and cast my eyes below me, to see how I might drop clear of the fore yard, at the same instant I directed my thought in prayer to Him, that was alone able to save, at that awful moment, a rope called the studding sail halliards flapped close to me, and knowing an opportunity like it might not occur again I let go my doubtful hold, and risked the siezure [*sic*] of it, which I providentially accomplished, and rapidly descended by it, safely upon the fore yard arm —when I found a rest for my foot, I was so weak, that my shipmates were obliged to come and assist me into the rigging, and by their aid, I got securely landed on deck to the great joy of myself, and the satisfaction of all who beheld me." Watson was now, you will remember, only between 15 and 16. The Admiral ordered the Fame to the Bay of Naples, where she stayed a few days; thence she went to Palermo. It had a good harbour, frequented by Sicilian frigates. Watson says that within half an hour of the Fame's arrival it was surrounded by boatloads of prostitutes, each boat with a fiddler or other musician. No difficulty seems to have been made about their admission on board; and Watson speaks with some disgust about their behaviour. He quotes Milton, too, describing them as

> Bred only, and completed to the taste
> Of lustful appetence; to sing, to dance,
> To dress, to troll the tongue, and roll the eye.

He comments, too, on their custom of going ashore every morning to get absolution from the priest, and then— returning in the evening!

After four days at Palermo, they returned to the fleet. One of the Fame's midshipmen was Lord Algernon Percy (afterwards Lord Prudhoe), son of the Duke of Northumberland; and Watson found him kindly, unaffected and dignified. They had talks about the North. Watson gives a vivid description of the motley crowd that went to make up a man-of-war's crew: they made an epitome of the world, and ranged from highwaymen, burglars, debauchees, to thread-worn beaux, jack-a-dandies, comedians, poets, painters; from the simple, honest tar to the man who had worn his 'purple and fine linen' and was as polite and cunning as a Chesterfield. There were all sorts, in fact, good and bad—the bad predominating. As winter approached, they again returned to Mahon, in Minorca. There, by Lord Collingwood's wish, divine service was held every Sunday. On the Fame, Captain Bennet officiated as chaplain to a more or less inattentive crew. Some of the men, instead of prayer books, would provide themselves with old popular histories or song-books; others would find a pretext for going aloft and so would escape attendance altogether; meanwhile the Captain's mistress would watch the proceedings from the windows under the poop.

The worst of the season being over, the Fame "put to sea again, and cruised off Toulon, as usual, doing nothing but tacking back and forward, from and to the land, watching the manœuvres of the French fleet, which sometimes came out of port to plague us, to make sail, and clear for battle, and then ran away from us like wild geese, giving us a wild goose chace after them beneath their batteries."

They returned to Minorca towards the end of the summer. Watson often saw "his Maria," and on one occasion got her to promise to come on board the next afternoon. While he was at dinner, however, eagerly expecting the time of her visit, they heard the report of a gun and then learnt, from the signals flying on a look-out frigate, that the French were out of Toulon and were steering for Barcelona. The

whole fleet immediately put to sea, and Watson's hopes and
dreams of Maria were ended. He never saw her again,
though, as he says, "her image clung to my breast, and for
years maintained its post there, in preference to all I ever
beheld, in a land of strangers."

After two or three days they came upon the French, who,
on seeing the strength of the English fleet, turned tail.
The English chased them for a day or two, but only seven of
the fastest 74's could come up with them and force their
rear into action. The Fame was a slow sailer and was out
of it. About six of the enemy's ships were driven on shore;
the rest made good their escape to Toulon. Soon afterwards Lord Collingwood died,[5] and Captain Bennet left the
Fame and went to England. Captain Hornby now commanded the ship for six months, and then, their time being
out for remaining on a foreign station, they were ordered
to Malta to take convoy to England. They were happy at
the idea of returning home after an absence of more than
three years. They lay at Malta for three or four months,
and were allowed to earn money by work in the Dockyard.
When a ship was returning, like the Fame, to England, it
was customary to fill up, from the men who had not originally left England with her, the crews needed for other
ships on the station. Watson, it will be remembered, had
only joined the Fame at Gibraltar; and so his name was
called for fresh service. Lieut. Norton, however, kindly got
him exempted, and had another sent in his place. But he
was soon called on again, men being wanted for the Eagle,
a 74. Norton was again ready to befriend him, but Watson
did not accept his offer, being unwilling that another man
should suffer for him. Accordingly, until the Eagle arrived,
he was sent on board the Trident. The Fame then sailed
for England.

Christmas Day arrived about a fortnight later. It fell
on a Sunday, and was celebrated too uproariously by Watson
and his mates. In their drunken insolence they defied the
authority of the marines and officers of the Trident, Watson
striking a corporal and pushing him down. The First
Lieutenant had three or four of them arrested, and dispersed

[5] 1810.

the mob.   Captain Vincent came on board next morning, and after reprimanding the rest of the Fame's men sent for Watson and his comrades.   He pointed out the gravity of their mutinous conduct, read the Articles of War, and told them that if he tried them by Court Martial they must inevitably be hanged, like many others for a less offence. However, he took into account their ignorance, their disappointment at being left behind by the Fame, and, in Watson's case, the good character he had received from the Fame.   He then, with an earnest warning, let them go; and his clemency was justified by their subsequent conduct. His kindness went further, for when six weeks later they were drafted on board the Eagle (under Captain Rowley) he recommended them as well disposed men, and did not mention the unfortunate episode.

On the Eagle Watson remained during the rest of his naval service.   He describes Captain Rowley as a good commander, rigid in discipline at sea, but considerate in port; he was, moreover, as a friend, beneficent and faithful. The First Lieutenant (Augustus Cannon), an Irishman, was brave, generous, a perfect seaman, and popular with all. The Second Lieutenant was steady, sober-minded, and a good officer.   Of the midshipmen one, named Moore, is warmly praised; another proved haughty, cowardly, revengeful: he was at once obsequious and tyrannical.   Watson calls him Hector, because he was so *un*like Homer's Hector.

The necessary repairs to the Eagle having been made, they left Malta for Corfu, "the Corcyra of the ancients" (as Watson is aware).   Here, relieving the Magnificent, a 74, they stayed for some months, cruising about and occasionally anchoring pretty close to the town, which was of course in French hands.   Watson henceforward had much active service in minor engagements, such as interrupting or destroying the enemy's commerce, taking prizes, and doing "cutting out" work.   They were occupied round about Corfu, or on the Albanian coast, or near Taranto, or among the Ionian Isles.   Zante in particular he describes, speaking among other things of the leathern wine-bottles in the shape of the animals from whose skins they were made.   On the

Albanian coast the men were often few in number, and
always lazy, most of the work of the fields being done by the
women, who were numerous.   Such men as there were were
mostly soldiers, loitering about the margin of the sea, and
looking formidable.   The little Island of Fano, off Corfu,
gave the Eagle a good deal of occupation.   It was garrisoned
by the French, who had built, on the margin of a small
inlet, a fort which covered the retreat of small craft when
pursued by the English barges.   Some French gun-boats
also lay there, which served as escorts to Corfu.   In one
scrap with them, "Hector's" cowardice was obvious.
Three of the Eagle's boats under Cannon, Greenfield and
"Hector" were trying to draw the gun-boats away from the
fort in order to board them.   In the ruse of retreating,
"Hector's" boat, in which Watson was, got left far behind the
others, being a clumsy pinnace.   As shots from the gun-
boats were flying over them, "Hector" urged the crew
to greater efforts, crying "pull away my dear fellows! O do!
for God's sake pull away."   The men were so pleased
with his fears that some of them said, "Let us pull gently to
punish the lubber."   The French, however, were afraid to
venture too far, and soon turned tail, fearing the trap.
The boats promptly swung round and gave chase, and
"Hector's" pinnace was again left behind.   This time,
the danger being past, his tone was very different.
"Pull away, you damned rascals," he cried, "pull
you lazy scoundrels!"   Nevertheless the gun boats reached
their creek in safety, and the boats returned to the
Eagle.

The Turks or Albanians supplied them well with provisions
and live stock, and the sailors made pets of some of the
animals, e.g. Billy the goat, Jenny the cow, Tom the sheep,
Jack the goose.   Jack in particular, from his comical ways,
was a great favourite.

Watson was, he says, now become "a proper man-of-
war's man.   I could drink, fight, swear, etc., etc., with
great eclat, and being often away at night, I was perfectly
inured to toil."   The toil, especially in the boats, was indeed
heavy.   Almost nightly they left the ship at 8.0, were
tugging at the oar till 3.0 or 4.0 in the morning, then perhaps

were engaged with the enemy for an hour or two, after which they returned to the ship, reaching it perhaps at 3.0 or 4.0 in the afternoon. Thus they only had about four hours for eating and sleeping. As a consequence Watson was always hungry and never felt "full" in spite of the liberal rations. Leaving Corfu after five or six months they went to Venice and Trieste on the same kind of work. Presently they returned to Fano, and captured a large Grecian polacca, loaded with French goods. This they sent off to Malta. Then they chased two frigates and a brig, in heavy weather. They let the brig go, although she struck her colours, and they held on after the frigates, the smaller of which, La Corceyre, they ultimately captured. There were about 300 on board her, including some troops for Corfu. Her also they sent off to Malta. The other frigate got away. Captain Rowley's official account of the capture of La Corceyre, dated Nov. 28, 1811, is quoted.

Watson's age, by the way, was now 19. A few days later two dangerous thunderstorms occurred. In the first the lightning struck the main-mast, and the hands who were taking in sail were knocked off the main top gallant yard. They were pitiably scorched, and tumbled into the top and cross-trees, and some of them were maimed for life. The sail was torn from the yard as clear as if cut by a knife or scissors; the strong iron hoops that bound the mast below the top were broken like flax. However, the mast stood. The second storm occurred three nights later, when Watson was at the mast head. He just managed to complete his job there and get down when the mast was again struck. It was "rent by the lightning, and it appeared like a bundle of disparting rods on fire without flame." They at once made for Cephalonia, where they got stores, and came in for an extraordinarily violent hurricane. After returning to Corfu again for a month or two, they went to Valona for provisions, etc. At Valona Watson had a row with an Irish "captain of the top," who was half-drunk, and who struck him and nearly knocked him overboard. Watson caught him by the neck and laid him on his back. For this he was harshly thrashed by Captain Rowley, and got the cat o' nine tails as well. Rowley did not however put his name in the black book. Soon afterwards Watson was nearly in another scrape with the bullying "Hector," but got out of the difficulty by playing "old soldier": he was sent to the sick bay, where he had a month's drastic treatment by the doctor, who apparently was no genius. The Eagle next went from Corfu to Venice and its neighbourhood. Near Trieste they carried off about 14 bullocks from a meadow in which they were grazing; payment was offered, but the peasants feared to take it from an enemy. A second attempt of the same kind was repulsed by a troop of cavalry. After reconnoitring between Trieste and Lissa, Captain Rowley decided to go and refit at Malta, from which they had been absent 14 months. But before they sailed they had one or two skirmishes, one of which is well described. Watson got a shot wound, and was off duty for about six weeks. On their way to Malta they touched at Fano (off Corfu), where one of their cutters, with 10 men and an officer, attacked and captured a French gun-boat with 30 men on board. The gun-boat had on board some wearing apparel for the wife of the Governor of Corfu. Captain Rowley despatched this to her, under a flag of truce, along with a hamper of English porter; and she responded by sending him a ketch laden with fresh beef, vegetables, soft bread, etc. So they parted good friends.

They soon reached Malta. Since they now had prize-money due to them they were welcomed with music and invitations to go on shore by the venal creatures of the port; and Watson gives a mock panegryric on the power of money. While the Eagle was being overhauled the men had a good deal of leave on shore. Watson came across a woman—English Nan he calls her—whose handsome, strapping grossness both attracted and repelled him. What with drink, however, and some resulting insubordination, he presently got confined on board ship during the rest of the stay at Malta.

En route now for the Adriatic, they stayed a few days at Messina, where the British Governor presented Captain Rowley with a fine boat, the Green Barge, which plays an important part in the rest of the story. Watson describes the Straits of Messina, and talks of Scylla and Charybdis, quoting Dryden's Virgil.

> Far on the right, her dogs foul Scylla hides:
> Charybdis roaring on the left presides,
> And in her greedy whirlpool sucks the tides,
> Then spouts them from below: with fury driven,
> The waves mount up, and wash the face of heaven.
> But Scylla from her den, with open jaws,
> The sinking vessel in her eddy draws,
> Then dashes on the rocks.

Watson goes on with some rather quaint classical references to Polyphemus, Cyclops, and the son of Laertes. He does not know "what has become of the Aborigines now," but supposes "they are with those giants, who lived before the flood, filling with their dust, some huge furrow in the 'valley of the shadow of death' . . . if ever they lived at all?"

Leaving Messina, they went to the upper Adriatic *via* Zante (where they took on board a detachment of the 35th Regiment of Foot). Watson comments on the distinction made between soldiers, marines and sailors. They now had numerous skirmishes, in which Watson, working in the Green Barge, bore his part. There were, for instance, the attacks on two batteries. The first had 8 cannons, and in this attack they failed, though, had they known it, they were within an ace of success. The second had 4 guns, and this they captured. Some of the sailors got hopelessly drunk: Watson in one house saw several of them "surrounding a large cask upon their knees, lapping up wine from it like dogs, or pigs." As none of them would follow him he left them and went on his way alone. Just before the fort was blown up he got his foot and right hand badly crushed by the carriage of a gun, and was away from the Green Barge for about three weeks.

Watson contrasts the fighting qualities of the Irish, Scotch, and English. He thinks the Irish daringly bold and impetuous, but requiring to be led; their spirit needs frequent working up by their leaders' influence. The Scot, he says, "is sullenly brave, and proud of the memory of his ancestors; he fights to maintain their renown, and ancient glories, and thinks himself only worthy of fame, as far as he imitates them." "As for John Bull, he is a mixture of both . . . he is resolute, and intrepid, and cooly [sic] courageous . . . he depends on none but himself; he thinks the battle his own, and endures its protraction, with a stubborn and un-equalled fortitude. . . . In short, he is what Lord Clarendon described Hampden to be, 'A man much to be desired for a friend, and much to be dreaded as an enemy.'"

In the next fight in which Watson took part he was severely wounded; and we have now reached the closing episode in his life as a seaman. This was the battle of Goro, in one of the mouths of the Po, 17 Sept. 1812, when Watson was just 20. It was one of those small engagements which are, as he and others held, far more exacting personally than general engagements of the fleets. He calls it, in a poem he wrote, The Battle of the Po.[6]

Three barges were concerned: the Green (in which was G. W.) was commanded by Cannon, the Red by Moore, and the White by Festing, a young lieutenant. They made ready (with ammunition, bread, wine, etc.) and left the Eagle at 8.0 p.m. on 16th Sept., being 28 miles from the land. The design was to reconnoitre the coast and inter-cept ships trading between Venice and Ancona. About midnight they reached a fleet of fishermen, who said they were about two miles from Goro; they added that a fort defended the entrance to the harbour, and that a gun-boat and several vessels were riding there. Lowering their sails they rowed near the shore and waited for daylight. They then saw that they were near the battery, which stood on an isthmus between them and the harbour, and that in addition to the ships there were some troopers on the beach who occasionally fired at them and then retired behind the mounds raised for their shelter. The fort guns did not fire, but more sharp-shooters were sent down to the beach. To avoid their shot Cannon sheered off a little, meaning to work abreast of the harbour, whereupon the gun-boat hauled from under the rampart and stood without the point and began firing so as to decoy them. Cannon, angry at the challenge, determined to attack her. The Red and White

[6] It is not given here, and so far as I am aware was never published.

Barges got stuck for a time on the sand banks, and diverted the fire of the fort from the Green, which made for the gunboat, and, after a sharp attack, boarded and captured her. By now Moore and Festing, having got their boats off unhurt, came up and congratulated the Greens on their success. That is the first scene in the drama.

As the battery was now firing on them they withdrew towards the other side of the harbour amidst some neutral Turkish ships, and the firing ceased. Looking round they espied and boarded, without opposition, a beautiful French latteen-rigged galley. Manning their two prizes with ten men from the Green Barge and one or two from each of the others, they proposed to rejoin their ship, and their only regret was that they had not three prizes, viz. one apiece. As they headed for the sea they noticed flags running up and down on various signal posts; the battery also re-opened fire and succeeded in drawing their attention and delaying them. Then they found that a fleet of 23 sail was standing in. At first they were delighted, thinking them to be merchantmen and an easy prey. The ships came rapidly on, formed a line across the entrance to the harbour, and completely blocked them in. Cannon's telescope now revealed that the three foremost were gun-boats—one apiece for the barges with a vengeance! The English sent the crews of their prizes on shore in the small boats, secured the officers below, and headed for the enemy, the Green Barge leading. When the firing began they found to their consternation that not only the three gun-boats were armed, but all the 23 vessels. To oppose this fleet they had only their badly manned open boats. They were at first appalled; but recovering courage they cheered and bent to their oars. Grape shot flew about them like hail, till the main mast of the Green Barge was chipped on every side, like a cabbage stalk eaten by caterpillars. Moore was quietly observing the ship he intended to board. Festing had sheered off out of the line of the gun-boats and was using his cannonade: he sank a vessel and threw others into confusion. The Green Barge was now in the enemy's line, and was exposed to the fire of two of the gunboats. Cannon asked Watson (who was near him) which they should attack, and they made for one with a white bottom, thinking she was the commodore. As they turned towards her she fired, and Cannon fell with two balls in his breast. He lay there during the rest of the engagement, asking from time to time how things went.[7] Moore was now summoned to take command, and came up instantly. Leaving the vessel that had wounded Cannon they swung alongside of another, which proved to be really the commodore. Watson, from his position, was the first to attempt the boarding; but in the act he and two others were hit by cannister shot from a gun at six foot range, and tumbled back into the boat. Two balls struck Watson, injuring one of his fingers and the bone of his right thigh. The ship was captured. In trying to get on board her Watson's thigh-bone snapped. Of the Green Barge's crew, five out of ten, as well as Cannon, had been wounded, each with two balls. The British now turned the bow gun of the commodore on the white-bottomed vessel, and she hauled down her flag after one raking. Similarly others were vanquished, till the whole 23 had submitted to the three comparatively small barges. The French hurried into their boats unhindered by the English, who, with their small numbers, were only too glad to get them out of the way. Two or three of the Eagle's men were put into each of the vessels.

Such was the Battle of the Po. The defeated French had outnumbered the English by 100, they had had 26 more cannon, and some of their ships had had crews of over 30 men.

The brave young wife of the French commander remained on deck and showed much kindness to the wounded. She dressed and bandaged Watson's wounds and did all that she could for him. On reaching the Eagle, the injured were taken to the sick bay, where it was found that the damage to Watson's leg was too high to allow of amputation. The captured ships, which had valuable loads of oil and brandy, were manned and sent under Moore's command to Lissa. A gale caused the loss of a good many of them, as well as 30 of Watson's mates; the rest arrived safely. Watson was glad to reach Lissa, as his wound was bad; he was delirious at times and was copiously bled. After a short stay there he

[7] He died a day or two later

H

was transferred in the Kingfisher to Malta, which he reached, more dead than alive, after a fortnight's passage. He lay in hospital for 18 months, and during 11 of them was never off his back, so slow was the thigh-bone in uniting. His patience and fortitude were praised by the surgeon and his assistant, who showed him much kindness. A young shipmate of his, Charley Frith, who had been similarly wounded, died after two months; and Watson expected to follow him. But Providence, as he thinks, was working by roundabout ways towards his reformation and happiness. He illustrates his belief from Shakespeare:—

> Many things, having full reference
> To one consent, may work contrariously;
> As many arrows, loosed several ways,
> Fly to one mark;
> As many several roads meet in one Town:
> As many fresh streams run in one self sea:
> As many lines close in the dial's centre,
> So may a thousand actions, once afoot,
> End in one purpose.[8]

He amused himself by reading, writing on a slate, drawing, making clothes for the nurse's child, etc. This nurse, by the way, had formerly been hostess of the canteen where he met English Nan.

Supervision in the hospital was extraordinarily lax. For instance, one night in Watson's ward a marine, whose brain was turned, left his own bed and went up to that of a nigger, stared at him, then began to laugh. The nigger awoke, saw in the taper's dim light the madman's face with its glaring eyes close above him, and bolted in terror from his bed. Pursued by the maniac he fled round and round the ward, crying lustily for help. Many others got up to intervene, and the place was in an uproar. The madman himself now fled in his turn, and took refuge under Watson's bed. Watson, in his weakness, lay trembling, expecting every moment to be thrown out and killed. However, the man was persuaded to come out, and was fastened down in his own bed. Watson got no more sleep that night. On another occasion two sailors, who had each lost an arm,

---

[8] *Henry V.*, I., 2.

were near Watson's bed bearing him company. One of them was a Newcastle man. Presently they began disputing, then fighting. In their struggle they overbalanced and crashed down upon Watson, snapping his thigh again, which was then beginning to unite. Watson did not explain to the doctor how the accident arose, for fear the sailors should be sent to the guardship. His thigh was reset, but was never so straight again. The sailors were much concerned at what they had done, and the Newcastle man especially, while in hospital, rendered Watson many services. Altogether Watson gives an interesting picture of life in the hospital: telling of the way the patients beguiled the time, the singing, the telling of tales, the disputes about the nurses, and so forth. Presently the influence of the chaplain of the hospital, who had been summoned to read prayers to a dying man, turned Watson to religious thoughts. He took to reading the Bible and such other religious books as he could procure. He gradually triumphed over the follies of his youth, and resolved, if ever he reached home, to be another man.

Captain Rowley's official report of the battle off the Po, which is here given, describes Watson and two others, who were severely wounded, merely as slightly wounded.

During Watson's stay the plague attacked Valette, where the hospital was, and raged terribly for nine months. Then, however, a new Governor, General Maitland, did much to suppress it. When Watson's ship, the Eagle, put in to Malta on her way to England, Captain Rowley, Moore, and others, came to visit him. The Captain gave him a recommendatory letter, and his shipmates brought a bag of Spanish dollars, which he shared with two of his fellows who had been kind to him in the hospital. Allen, the surgeon, would not yet allow him to go to England. Watson was bitterly disappointed, and began to lose courage; but the sight of a young sailor who was brought in with both his arms shot off taught him that his lot might have been worse. He plucked up heart again, and hopped about on his crutches without further repining. At last Allen sanctioned his departure, and he sailed on the Repulse, a 74, which was to take a convoy to England. The change from hospital to the sick bay of a man-of-war was very trying. The young doctor, an inexperienced "saw-bones," promptly wanted to amputate his leg; but Watson trusted the judgment of the hospital surgeon, and refused. They had a tedious passage of nearly two months. When about 100 miles from England they met two frigates with flags flying from every masthead: peace had been declared with France. At last they saw, with indescribable pleasure, the white cliffs of Britain. Watson apostrophises his "much loved country," and quotes Thomson:—

> Island of bliss! amid the subject seas
> That thunder round the rocky coasts, set up
> At once the wonder, terror, and delight
> Of distant nations, whose remotest shore
> Can soon be shaken by thy Naval arm,
> Not to be shook thyself; but all assaults
> Baffling, like thy hoar cliffs the loud sea wave.

Passing Eddystone's tower they entered Plymouth Sound. Watson stayed at the hospital for more than a month, but was allowed to view the town, and notices that the foundations of the Breakwater were then being laid. The hospital nurses, strange as it now seems, were chiefly of "the frail sisterhood," and Watson had much ado to keep clear of them. He at first thought them simple and kind, but discovering their true colours, was careful to avoid them.

He left Plymouth before he was cured, at the urgent desire of his mother. He got his pay—over £120—and reached London in two days. There it took him a week to get his business affairs settled; e.g. he had to go down to Greenwich and arrange about his pension. But at last all was done. He got a seat in the Highflyer coach, which in due course set him down in Collingwood Street, Newcastle, in July, 1814. He found the place so much changed as to be unrecognisable. Getting presently to his mother's house, he found that she was out at an uncle's; and one of the neighbours went to tell her of her son's arrival. "The poor old lady," he says, "could scarcely believe the tidings, having been so often disappointed. When she came she gazed at me with surprise, and even doubted, whether I was in reality her child or not, for I did not appear to be the once rosy cheeked boy, that had left her ten years before; but having examined my chin, whereon was a particular mark, she was satisfied, and embraced me with . . . extacy [*sic*]." Other relations and friends soon arrived, and the evening of their reunion was spent in the greatest happiness.

Here Watson's *Narrative* ends. Of his subsequent life there seems to be no record. His book was published some 13 years later, in 1827. Meanwhile he must have worked diligently at self-education, for his first school-teaching, as we have seen, was of the briefest duration and most elementary character. He did not of course attain literary elegance, and his spelling and punctuation are very often queer. Yet he had a seeing eye, and could express himself with picturesque vigour; he could moreover quote effectively from some of the poets, amongst whom he seems to have admired Shakespeare, Milton, Thomson, Dryden, and Watts. On the whole one thinks of him as a courageous, thoughtful, and honest young Novocastrian.

Nature and Human Nature:

An Inquiry based chiefly on Wordsworth.[1]

> Qui mérite mieux notre dévotion, d'un
> paysage et d'un beau monument ou d'une noble
> figure humaine? La splendeur morale et qui
> se suffit à elle-même, est-elle d'un ordre supér-
> ieur à cette autre splendeur qui a besoin de la
> matière et qui se manifeste par des lignes d'hori-
> zon ou des façonnements de marbre? Ou
> plutôt n'est-ce pas la même, et, si nous con-
> cevions la beauté comme elle doit être conçue,
> c'est-à-dire, toujours et partout, comme un
> *mystère spirituel*, n'apercevrions-nous pas une
> profonde unité d'origine sous ses innombrables
> formes, si différentes soient-elles d'apparence?
>
> BOURGET, *Sensations d'Italie.*

IT may well be that a good many of us hold in a general
way, with Pope, that "the proper study of mankind is man."
Yet occasions arise when one is moved to examine, either
afresh or more carefully than hitherto, the source of the
fascination which external nature, whether at first hand or
in descriptions, undoubtedly exercises both upon ourselves
and upon others.

In our customary habit of thought the scientist, busy with
his geological specimens, or poring over microscopic struc-
tures, or lost in his study of the stars, or measuring physical
forces (like the faint heat thrown out by a candle 50 feet
away), may perhaps seem to be working almost outside
the pale of human interests. True, these studies may be
used ultimately, by men who are gifted with practical as
well as theoretical acumen, to promote the prosperity or the

[1] Read to the English Association (Newcastle Branch) in 1913.

safety or the health of mankind; but it is at least questionable how far these practical applications at all inspire or control the theoretical study. Generally the knowledge would appear to be sought for its own sake; and to us it may have the appearance of being cold and inhuman knowledge.

We shall receive perhaps the same sort of impression if we go into a museum and there walk about looking at the variety of life-like birds and beasts. We shall think they are very skilfully arranged, and shall for a time admire their perfect poise and their attitudes and colours; but will not this aesthetic pleasure be presently exhausted? Unless we are ourselves students of zoology, our first contentment will probably soon be followed by mental lassitude. The objects, though they may be indeed beautiful, are outside our customary ways of thought and seem unrelated to vital human interests. So we shall praise the naturalists who have gathered and mounted the specimens with so much ingenuity and patience, and say they have doubtless displayed them with much accuracy and understanding; and at last shall make our escape feeling a little baffled and depressed.

In kind if not in degree the experience may recall to our mind, if we are fiction readers, the feelings of a practical sportsman described in a book published some years ago. A man called Growse, whose interests all centre in his bag, is out shooting in an Indian jungle. His companion is Wade, who besides his love of sport is keenly alive to the beauties of nature. This love of nature is not very intelligible to Growse. "Why," privately queried he, "should any one *like* to stare at water or dew with the moon shining on it? And what particular pleasure could there be in seeing the flash of a golden auriole's wing in the sunlight, or watching the flight of a paradise fly-catcher, with its long floating tail? The birds were pretty enough, no doubt, but they were not game birds, and one couldn't shoot them for sport, though one might do so for a collection. No, beyond appreciating the excellent fact that it sheltered wild animals for him to kill, Mr. Growse could perceive none of those 'joys and delights' of the jungle that Wade had once spoken of in a burst of confidence when they first became acquainted. He supposed it must be those mysterious delights that rendered so fine a shot as Wade unruffled by the ill-luck of a blank day."[2]

If, however, it is rather on the poets that our mind runs, we shall be disposed to admit, with a half satirical quip of regret for ourselves, how "little we see in nature that is ours." We shall recall too what Wordsworth says of sunset beauties and clouds:—

> They are of the sky,
> And from our earthly memories fade away.

Or again we shall have to agree for the nonce that

> Grove, isle, with every shape of sky-built dome,
> Though clad in colours beautiful and pure,
> Find in the heart of man no natural home:
> The immortal mind craves objects that endure.

Thoughts more or less like these may be at the back of our minds as we emerge from the museum, or leave the house of our geologist or astronomer. Yet, after all, our sense of baffled dissatisfaction may lead us to further inquiry. Why is it that to ourselves, as to a large portion of mankind, such things are so deeply interesting? "The proper study of mankind . . ." Well, what of the very poets themselves—a pre-eminently human race, whose works assuredly come within our purview as a "proper study"? Why is it worth their while, presumably, to describe actual scenes of nature?—solitary clouds or clouds in massed ranges, the flight of birds, the sound of great winds, sunlight seen through green leaves, white sheets of water, stars, flowers, streams? Take the definite case of Wordsworth himself. As we fix our thoughts upon him, or turn his pages, one instance after another confronts us. Sometimes it is flowers alone that he describes, either in passing mention, as in this:—

> There bloomed the strawberry of the wilderness;
> The trembling eyebright showed her sapphire blue,
> The thyme her purple;

[2] Perrin's *A Free Solitude*, pp. 51-2.

or else in greater elaboration, as in the famous piece about
daffodils:—

> All at once I saw a crowd,
> A host, of golden daffodils;
> Beside the lake, beneath the trees,
> Fluttering and dancing in the breeze.
> Continuous as the stars that shine
> And twinkle on the milky way,
> They stretched in never-ending line
> Along the margin of a bay:
> Ten thousand saw I at a glance,
> Tossing their heads in sprightly dance.

Sometimes it is birds and flowers together, depicted in an
exquisite sunny group that is all a-quiver with gleams of
colour and with lovely darting motion:—

> Beneath these fruit-tree boughs that shed
> Their snow-white blossoms on my head,
> With brightest sunshine round me spread
> Of spring's unclouded weather,
> In this sequestered nook how sweet
> To sit upon my orchard-seat!
> And birds and flowers once more to greet,
> My last year's friends together.
>
> One have I marked, the happiest guest
> In all this covert of the blest:
> Hail to Thee, far above the rest
> In joy of voice and pinion!
> Thou, Linnet! in thy green array,
> Presiding Spirit here to-day,
> Dost lead the revels of the May;
> And this is thy dominion. . . .
>
> Amid yon tuft of hazel trees
> That twinkle to the gusty breeze,
> Behold him perched in ecstasies,
> Yet seeming still to hover;
> There! where the flutter of his wings
> Upon his back and body flings
> Shadows and sunny glimmerings,
> That cover him all over.
>
> My dazzled sight he oft deceives,
> A Brother of the dancing leaves . . .

Then, how Wordsworth loves to describe water—now pointing to clear mirror-like stretches, as of

> This hornéd bay
> Whose amorous water multiplies
> The flitting halcyon's vivid dyes;
> And smooths her liquid breast—to show
> These swan-like specks of mountain snow;

now dwelling with delight on the alternate pools and turmoil of some running brook, where one may espy

> Shade upon the sunshine lying
>   Faint and somewhat pensively;
> And downward Image gaily vying
>   With its upright living tree
> Mid silver clouds, and openings of blue sky. . . .

anon turning elsewhere

> To mark its eddying foam-balls prettily distrest
> By ever-changing shape and want of rest;
>   Or watch . . .
>   The current as it plays
> In flashing leaps and stealthy creeps
>   Adown a rocky maze;
> Or note (translucent summer's happiest chance!)
> In the slope-channel floored with pebbles bright,
> Stones of all hues, gem emulous of gem.

At another time he will conjure up a glimmering lake set among trees in some lonely twilight scene, when

> the earliest stars begin
> To move along the edges of the hills,

and he will make us hear the noise of birds roused by a lad who

> Blew mimic hootings to the silent owls,
> That they might answer him.—And they would shout
> Across the watery vale, and shout again,
> Responsive to his call,—with quivering peals,
> And long halloos, and screams, and echoes loud
> Redoubled and redoubled; concourse wild
> Of jocund din! And when there came a pause
> Of silence . . .

. . . . . . a gentle shock of mild surprise
Has carried far into his heart the voice
Of mountain-torrents; or the visible scene
Would enter unawares into his mind
With all its solemn imagery, its rocks,
Its woods, and that uncertain heaven received
Into the bosom of the steady lake.

And as he lingers on flowers and birds and water, so likewise trees and woods are continually in his pages. For instance, there is this noteworthy description of a sequestered grove of hazel trees:—

O'er pathless rocks,
Through beds of matted fern, and tangled thickets,
Forcing my way, I came to one dear nook
Unvisited, where not a broken bough
Drooped with its withered leaves, ungracious sign
Of devastation; but the hazels rose
Tall and erect, with tempting clusters hung.
A virgin scene! A little while I stood,
Breathing with such suppression of the heart
As joy delights in.

Or, still better, there is the wonderful picture of Airey-Force Valley. In it, besides water and trees, there is a distant effect of wind playing on a solitary ash, with the unheard melodies which its rhythmic motion can suggest. But at first all is still.

Not a breath of air
Ruffles the bosom of this leafy glen.
From the brook's margin, wide around, the trees
Are steadfast as the rocks; the brook itself,
Old as the hills that feed it from afar,
Doth rather deepen than disturb the calm
Where all things else are still and motionless.
And yet, even now, a little breeze, perchance
Escaped from boisterous winds that rage without,
Has entered, by the sturdy oaks unfelt,
But to its gentle touch how sensitive
Is the light ash! that pendent from the brow
Of yon dim cave, in seeming silence makes
A soft eye-music of slow-waving boughs,
Powerful almost as vocal harmony
To stay the wanderer's steps and soothe his thoughts.

How the magic of sunlight, too, illuminates scene after scene. One instance, beyond what has already been recalled, is this, where a stormy night is followed by a brilliant morning, and where a hare is seen running in a little glory of sun-caught mist.

> The birds are singing in the distant woods;
> Over his own sweet voice the Stock-dove broods;
> The Jay makes answer as the Magpie chatters;
> And all the air is filled with pleasant noise of waters.
> All things that love the sun are out of doors;
> The sky rejoices in the morning's birth;
> The grass is bright with rain-drops;—on the moors
> The hare is running races in her mirth;
> And with her feet she from the plashy earth
> Raises a mist, that, glittering in the sun,
> Runs with her all the way, wherever she doth run.

But of the other aspects of nature in which for their own sake Wordsworth delighted—stars, mountains, valleys, and so forth—it would take too long to speak in detail.

So far as we have gone, then, the things and scenes described are described, it would seem, simply because of the joy in them that Wordsworth felt. There is little or no intention to use them by way of illustrating his pictures of humanity or his creations of mythologic fancy. They are not used as similes, nor as the manifestations of personified powers, such as Nature, or the like. To what purpose, then, does he apply them? and wherein does the pleasure which he (and we) derive from them consist? Do they afford, fundamentally, a physiological contentment of eye and ear and nostril—or, to speak more strictly, a suggestion and recollection of such contentment, so vividly recalled as to have almost the effect of actual experience? Certainly we imagine ourselves in the midst of these scenes; they satisfy our sense of colour and form; and for the time they occupy all our thoughts. They afford us pleasant relief by distracting us from mental anxieties or serious human cares. We can store them in our minds, and recall them at will when jaded or sleepless, dwelling on them till the physiological balance is restored. So, being re-invigorated (as after other physical recreations, like open air, rest, exercise), we can resume our customary occupations. If however

such scenes were considerably prolonged, should we come
to feel, in this case also, that they needed to be
brought more directly into touch with our human experience, and our normal ways of thought? Is it in this
sort of half curative way that Wordsworth and those akin
to him look upon external Nature? Is this the secret of the
fascination exercised upon them by her quiet beauties and
her mighty forces? Do they value her as affording an escape
from human ills—as Shelley, for instance, says:—

> I love snow and all the forms
>> Of the radiant frost.
> I love waves and winds, and storms.
>> Every thing almost
> Which is Nature's, and may be
> Untainted by man's misery.

Such a view of nature, and such a use of her scenes, may
doubtless often be found in Wordsworth; and examples
will not be far to seek. To begin with there is the well-
known invocation of sleep:—

> A flock of sheep that leisurely pass by,
> One after one; the sound of rain, and bees
> Murmuring; the fall of rivers, winds and seas,
> Smooth fields, white sheets of water, and pure sky;
> I have thought of all by turns, and yet do lie
> Sleepless. . . .
> Even thus last night, and two nights more, I lay,
> And could not win thee, Sleep! by any stealth. . . .

Then there is the description of Grasmere Lake: its quiet
beauties afford him an exquisite relief from his sombre
brooding on the wildness of human passions:—

> Clouds, lingering yet, extend in solid bars
> Through the grey west; and lo! these waters, steeled
> By breezeless air to smoothest polish, yield
> A vivid repetition of the stars;
> Jove, Venus, and the ruddy crest of Mars
> At happy distance from earth's groaning field,
> Where ruthless mortals wage incessant wars.
> . . . If unholy deeds
> Ravage the world, tranquillity is here!

Once more, it is to the lovely scenery around Tintern Abbey that he has owed, he says:—

> In hours of weariness, sensations sweet,
> Felt in the blood. . . .
> And passing even into my purer mind,
> With tranquil restoration. . . .
> . . . . . Not less, I trust,
> To them I may have owed . . . that blessed mood,
> In which the burthen of the mystery,
> In which the heavy and the weary weight
> Of all this unintelligible world
> Is lightened.

Think, too, of his address to Wansfell:—

> How oft, to elevate our spirits, shone
> Thy visionary majesties of light,
> How in thy pensive glooms our hearts found rest.

What a penetrating change, moreover, is wrought in him when he hears the cuckoo's simple re-iterated note. He can throw aside the burden of years like a garment and re-capture the vivid, golden days of his childhood! He addresses the bird thus:—

> Thou bringest unto me a tale
> Of visionary hours. . . .
> And I can listen to thee yet;
> Can lie upon the plain
> And listen, till I do beget
> That golden time again.
> O blessèd Bird! the earth we pace
> Again appears to be
> An unsubstantial, faery place.

These examples are enough to show that the use of country scenes and of external nature as an escape from the ills that man is heir to was a familiar one to Wordsworth. That this was the whole of the matter, however, can hardly be said; for in any case such employment of them is a grown-up affair, whereas Wordsworth's delight in them dates from his first youth, if not from his very childhood. His feelings and attitude towards "lonely nature" from childhood to early manhood are sufficiently revealed by himself in the

two following passages. The first is from the *Excursion*
(Book I.) and is as follows:—

> He attained
> An active power to fasten images
> Upon his brain; and on their pictured lines
> Intensely brooded, even till they acquired
> The liveliness of dreams.
> Nor did he fail,
> While yet a child, with a child's eagerness
> Incessantly to turn his ear and eye
> On all things which the moving seasons brought
> To feed such appetite. . . .

> But for the growing Youth
> What soul was his, when, from the naked top
> Of some bold headland, he beheld the sun
> Rise up, and bathe the world in light! He looked—
> Ocean and earth, the solid frame of earth
> And ocean's liquid mass, in gladness lay
> Beneath him. . . .

> Sound needed none,
> Nor any voice of joy; his spirit drank
> The spectacle: sensation, soul, and form,
> All melted into him; they swallowed up
> His animal being; in them did he live,
> And by them did he live; they were his life.

In such wise, speaking ostensibly of the Wanderer whom he
met (though, as the Preface indicates, really of himself)
he describes how nature from the first held him under
her spell. Of himself a little later, too (as a youth of 23),
he speaks in Tintern Abbey—revisited in 1798 (when he was
28).

> Nature then . . .
> To me was all in all. I cannot paint
> What then I was. The sounding cataract
> Haunted me like a passion: the tall rock,
> The mountain, and the deep and gloomy wooa,
> Their colours and their forms, were then to me
> An appetite; a feeling and a love,
> That had no need of a remoter charm,
> By thought supplied, nor any interest
> Unborrowed from the eye.

This, of course, is not the language of one who turns to nature and to external forms and colours as a pleasant alternative from his proper work as a man, or as an anodyne for *Welt-Schmerz*, or as a resource for winning sleep "by any stealth" when he is too wakeful.   Such healing use is indeed one way in which nature can be brought into relation with human thought and experience; but it is obviously not the whole solution of the matter. It would seem after all possible that, in what we call "external" nature—at all events as seen by Wordsworth and those like-minded with him—there may be something more intimately akin to what we call "human" nature—the human concerns which are said to be "the proper study of mankind." If to our human poets Nature can give such food for thought and even for haunting passion, surely there must be some bond penetrating and uniting the two worlds (of the "human" and of the "natural") which we have so far been disposed to regard as separate and almost incommensurable. What reconciliation between the two does Wordsworth make? Leaving aside the merely descriptive poems, how does he introduce nature into poems that are either concerned with definite human beings or that exhibit creative fancy and constructive imagination? Perhaps the simplest form of such introduction is by way of similes, as where, speaking of his sister Dorothy he says, with startling beauty of effect,

> Where'er my footsteps turned
> Her voice was like a hidden bird that sang,
> The thought of her was like a flash of light
> Or an unseen companionship,—a breath
> Of fragrance independent of the wind.

Or one may recall the admirable similes he employed to portray the motionless leech-gatherer whom he found beside a pool in a lonely place—"the oldest man he seemed that ever wore grey hairs":—

> As a huge stone is sometimes seen to lie
> Couched on the bald top of an eminence;
> Wonder to all who do the same espy,
> By what means it could thither come, and whence;
> So that it seems a thing endued with sense:

Like a sea-beast crawled forth, that on a shelf
Of rock or sand reposeth, there to sun itself;
Such seemed this Man, not all alive nor dead,
Nor all asleep—in his extreme old age.

Again, to exhibit the desolation caused by a friend's long silence, there is this marvellous comparison—so poignant, yet so simple:—

Why art thou silent . . .
Speak—though this soft warm heart, once free to hold
A thousand tender pleasures, thine and mine,
Be left more desolate, more dreary cold
Than a forsaken bird's-nest filled with snow
'Mid its own bush of leafless eglantine—
Speak, that my torturing doubts their end may know!

How delicately, too, by means of quiet natural beauties he can hint the blithe serenity and elusive charm of maidenhood! This, for example:—

She shall lean her ear
In many a secret place
Where rivulets dance their wayward round,
And beauty born of murmuring sound
Shall pass into her face.

Or this of another, who was like

A violet by a mossy stone
Half hidden from the eye!
—Fair as a star, when only one
Is shining in the sky.

Elsewhere a child, in her ever-renewed vitality and merriment, is likened to

the soft breeze ruffling the meadow-flowers,
Or from before it chasing wantonly
The many-coloured images imprest
Upon the bosom of a placid lake.

Or take this, to represent by the swaying buoyancy of a wave a maiden's exquisite grace of free movement:—

No fountain from its rocky cave
E'er tripped with foot so free;
She seemed as happy as a wave
That dances on the sea.

In another vein, in order to suggest the character of a proud man, not without nobility of aims and character, but soured by neglect, we are shown the desolate shore of Esthwaite, which he haunted, and the gloomy boughs of a lonely yew-tree under which he was wont to linger:—

> Here he loved to sit,
> His only visitants a straggling sheep,
> The stone-chat, or the glancing sand-piper:
> And on these barren rocks, with fern and heath,
> And juniper and thistle, sprinkled o'er,
> Fixing his downcast eye, he many an hour
> A morbid pleasure nourished, tracing here
> An emblem of his own unfruitful life.

To suggest, however, the greatness of a different man—Milton—it is to nature's silent heights and booming depths that he turns:—

> Thy soul was like a star, and dwelt apart:
> Thou hadst a voice whose sound was like the sea:
> Pure as the naked heavens, majestic, free,
> So didst thou travel on life's common way.

The nightingale's song is to Wordsworth emblematic of the wooing of "a creature of a 'fiery heart'":—

> These notes of thine—they pierce and pierce;
> Tumultuous harmony and fierce! . . .
> A song in mockery and despite
> Of shades, and dews, and silent night;
> And steady bliss, and all the loves
> Now sleeping in these peaceful groves.

By means of the stock-dove, on the other hand, he characterises a different wooing:—

> He did not cease; but cooed—and cooed;
> And somewhat pensively he wooed:
> He sang of love, with quiet blending,
> Slow to begin, and never ending.

Similes such as these of dancing waves, of lonely stars, of hidden birdsong, of resounding seas, avail in Wordsworth's hands to open up vistas of extraordinary suggestiveness. Their sudden revelations of delicacy and beauty and power give us a deeper insight into human nature. They show

us how marvellously man is poised in a mighty world, and
with what lovely faculties he is gifted. And so we find that
this way of similitude is one mode by which Wordsworth
brings his knowledge of "unhumanised" nature into relation
with mankind, suggesting to our minds in turn serene
beauties, sunny laughter, the play of changing moods, utter
silence, and the operation of vast, relentless force. These
"natural" similes, in fact, go to the building of great
"human" literature; and, if only for the sake of understanding that literature and of realising its power and
appropriateness, we shall be fain ourselves to observe
and study the ways of "lonely nature."

But it soon becomes apparent that this employment of
similes is not the only way in which Wordsworth relates
nature to man. The half mythological creations of his
fancy, the anthropomorphic way in which he personalises
her phenomena,[3] cannot fail to be observed. He felt

> The presences of Nature in the sky
> And on the earth; the visions of the hills,
> And Souls of lonely places.

That these two modes—similitude, and personification—
are at times not far from merging into one another, will
indeed be evident; but in the main they are clearly separable.
Let us look at some more definite examples of the latter
mode. Perhaps one of the simplest cases occurs in his
address to the Daisy:—

> A nun demure of lowly port;
> Or sprightly maiden, of Love's court;
> In thy simplicity the sport
>   Of all temptations;
> A queen in crown of rubies drest;
> A starveling in a scanty vest;
> Are all, as seems to suit thee best
>   Thy appellations.
> A little Cyclops with one eye
> Staring to threaten and defy,
> That thought comes next . . .

---

[3] One does not mean of course that he consciously and deliberately sets
about translating the one into the other, as one might turn things from
one language into another; but that his instinctive way was very often to
use the natural incidents, with which his mind was so richly stored, as a
means of expressing what we are wont to regard as especially human
concerns.

and so on. Similarly, the cuckoo is to him an ideal being,

> No bird, but an invisible thing,
> A voice, a mystery.

In the Ode to May we have a more elaborated creation.
Our thoughts perhaps will revert to the opening lines of
Lucretius, where Venus is addressed as the quickening
goddess of universal growth and of all the new year's glad
life.   To Wordsworth May comes as

> . . . the expected Power,
> Whose first-drawn breath, from bush and tree,
>   Shakes off that pearly shower.
> All Nature welcomes Her whose sway
>   Tempers the year's extremes;
> Who scattereth lustres o'er noon-day,
>   Like morning's dewy gleams. . . .
> Time was, blest Power! when youths and maids
>   At peep of dawn would rise,
> And wander forth, in forest-glades
>   Thy birth to solemnise. . . .
> Thy feathered Lieges bill and wings
>   In love's disport employ;
> Warmed by thy influence, creeping things
>   Awake to silent joy;
> Queen art thou still for each gay plant
>   Where the slim wild deer roves;
> And served in depths where fishes haunt
>   Their own mysterious groves.

Another example, in which a peaceful evening and a swaying
ocean are invested with the half-human, half-divine attri-
butes of serenity and unconquerable might, may be taken
from one of the sonnets:—

> It is a beauteous evening, calm and free,
> The holy time is quiet as a Nun
> Breathless with adoration; the broad sun
> Is sinking down in its tranquillity;
> The gentleness of heaven broods o'er the Sea:
> Listen! the mighty Being is awake,
> And doth with his eternal motion make
> A sound like thunder—everlastingly.

What is Wordsworth's idea of a Brook, again?   He contrasts
its quiet gaiety and permanence with human turmoil and
evanescence, and presents it as an almost personal being.
In a mode that is half-mythological and half-pantheistic
he addresses it thus:—

> It seems the Eternal Soul is clothed in thee
> With purer robes than those of flesh and blood,
> And hath bestowed on thee a safer good;
> Unwearied joy, and life without its cares.

And again:—

> Still glides the Stream, and shall for ever glide;
> The Form remains, the Function never dies;
> While we, the brave, the mighty, and the wise,
> We Men, who in our morn of youth defied
> The elements, must vanish.

Then there is that ode to the Clouds, which he represents
variously as a wingèd host, companions of the gale, children
of the sun, a wide-spread army, an endless flight of birds
migrating—

> Or rather do ye urge
> In caravan your hasty pilgrimage
> To pause at last on more aspiring heights
> Than these, and utter your devotion there
> With thunderous voice.

The poem is too long to quote, but as for other reasons, so
also in this connection, it well repays examination.   Incidentally we get this figure of the Wind:—

> The mountain blast
> Shall be our *hand* of music; he shall sweep
> The rocks and quivering trees, and billowy lake,
> And search the fibres of the caves, and they
> Shall answer.

In the magnificent poem on the Simplon Pass we get a
more universal representation of Nature—a marshalling of
her separate forces, and a swift upgathering and trans-
mutation of them into membership with her great single life.

                    The immeasurable height
Of woods decaying, never to be decayed,
The stationary blasts of waterfalls,
And in the narrow rent, at every turn
Winds thwarting winds bewildered and forlorn,
The torrents shooting from the clear blue sky,
The rocks that muttered close upon our ears,
Black drizzling crags that spake by the wayside
As if a voice were in them, the sick sight
And giddy prospect of the raving stream,
The unfettered clouds and region of the heavens,
Tumult and peace, the darkness and the light—
Were all like workings of one mind, the features
Of the same face, blossoms upon one tree,
Characters of the great Apocalypse,
The types and symbols of Eternity,
Of first, and last, and midst, and without end.

Turning to a quieter and simpler case, one may recall, in the description of a nutting expedition, the virgin grove of trees that the boy explores, with its running stream and its flowers. The devastation that the lad wrought may be touched upon, since it leads to the poet's view of the wood as inhabited by, or rather as embodying, an almost personal being. After the ruthless gathering of the spoil there supervened

                    The sense of pain when I beheld
The silent trees, and saw the intruding sky.—
Then, dearest Maiden, move along these shades
In gentleness of heart; with gentle hand
Touch—for there is a spirit in the woods.

A somewhat different example of Wordsworth's use of personification is that in which he regards Law (or Duty, according to the title he gives the poem) as guiding and ruling two realms: the "human" realm and the "natural." It is convenient for the moment to distinguish between them, as he himself places them side by side. The governance of the natural realm he illustrates thus:—

Flowers laugh before thee on their beds,
And fragrance in thy footing treads;
Thou dost preserve the stars from wrong;
And the most ancient heavens, through Thee, are fresh
    and strong.

Then, what of the far-reaching powers of gentle Spring?
The new vitality which she pours throughout her blithe
domain can penetrate the hearts not only of the young
but also of those whose years are mellowing:—

> She, who incites the frolic lambs
> In presence of their heedless dams,
> And to the solitary fawn
> Vouchsafes her lessons, bounteous Nymph
> That wakes the breeze, the sparkling lymph
> Doth hurry to the lawn;
> She, who inspires that strain of joyance holy
> Which the sweet Bird, misnamed the melancholy,
> Pours forth in shady groves, shall plead for me;
> And vernal mornings opening bright
> With views of undefined delight,
> And cheerful songs, and suns that shine
> On busy days, with thankful nights, be mine.

Spring is shown once more (in the Ode to Lycoris) as

> the Guest
> Whose smiles, diffused o'er land and sea,
> Seem to recall the Deity
> Of youth into the breast:
> May pensive Autumn ne'er present
> A claim to her disparagement!
> While blossoms and the budding spray
> Inspire us in our own decay;
> Still, as we nearer draw to life's dark goal,
> Be hopeful Spring the favourite of the Soul.

The above examples may serve to show how Wordsworth,
by way of simile and personification, employs the phenomena of nature to illuminate his studies both of concrete
men and women, and of abstract ideas. The qualities of
men are enhanced and beautified by his similes from nature;
the rule and laws of nature are humanised by his personi-
fications. The rich interweaving of the "natural" and the
"human," which he achieves, of itself lends attractiveness
to his view (which develops more clearly as one reads)
that there is an underlying unity wherein the one group
of things and the other may be reconciled.

Hitherto we have chiefly laid stress on Wordsworth's
preoccupation with lonely nature and the way in which,

amid the cares and difficulties of life, he turned back to it
for relief and refreshment; and we have likewise dwelt on
his similes and his more or less mythological creations
(of winds, clouds, spring, law). It may therefore have
seemed that the distinctively human side of things has
been, so far, incidental rather than dominant, and has
occupied a somewhat minor place in his mind. Yet his
interest in man and man's standing in the world was an
intense one; and as it has an important bearing on this
inquiry it is fitting to remind ourselves of it and to lay some
brief emphasis upon it. The growth of his profound concern
with humanity was due, partly at least, to his love of natural
scenes. He got to love country folk and their ways

> Not verily
> For their own sakes, but for the fields and hills
> Where was their occupation and abode.

So it was that he came into personal sympathy with the
shepherds, the dwellers in the Valley; and the tales of their
lives—such tales for instance as that of old Michael—won
steadily upon him. Apart from merely picturesque qualities,
such incidents as a waterspout that brings down half a
mountain, a May storm with loads of January snow killing
in one night twenty score of sheep, ice breaking up and
sweeping away a bridge, are associated intimately with the
welfare of the inhabitants: they make the real chronology
of their lives. The wild or tranquil countryside becomes
the scene of human happiness or human tragedy, and he
learned

> To look on nature, not as in the hour
> Of thoughtless youth; but hearing oftentimes
> The still sad music of humanity.

Even the transitory clouds, with their remote, unearthly
beauty came to suggest the swift passing of the lives of men:
clouds that are fled

> Down to the unapproachable abyss,
> Down to that hidden gulf from which they rose
> To vanish—fleet as days and months and years,
> Fleet as the generations of mankind,
> Power, glory, empire, as the world itself,
> The lingering world, when time hath ceased to be.

Of the chronological facts of his life, of the enlarging and deepening of his human experience, of the searching influence upon him, for instance, of the struggles and passions of the French Revolution, there is here no call to speak; but that these things ate into his mind, and tormented the inmost chords of his being, becomes very clear in passage after passage of his poetry. His outlook on nature, and his interpretation of her, became greatly modified by the new forces that from one reason and another stirred within him. This may be seen, to take one instance, in the stanzas suggested by a picture of Peele Castle. He had been living near the castle for a time in earlier days when all was in a state of quiet summer calm:—

> I saw thee every day; and all the while
> Thy Form was sleeping on a glassy sea.
> So pure the sky, so quiet was the air!
>
> . . .
> I could have fancied that the mighty Deep
> Was even the gentlest of all gentle Things.
> Ah! Then, if mine had been the Painter's hand,
> To express what then I saw: and add the gleam,
> The light that never was, on sea or land,
> The consecration, and the Poet's dream
>
> . . .
> A Picture had it been of lasting ease,
> Elysian quiet, without toil or strife. . . .
> So once it would have been,—'tis so no more;
> I have submitted to a new control:
> A power is gone, which nothing can restore;
> A deep distress hath humanised my Soul.
> Not for a moment could I now behold
> A smiling sea, and be what I have been.
>
> . . .
> Then, Beaumont, . . .
> This work of thine I blame not, but commend;
> This sea in anger, and that dismal shore.
> O 'tis a passionate Work!—yet wise and well,
> Well chosen is the spirit that is here;
> That Hulk which labours in the deadly swell,
> This rueful sky, this pageantry of fear!
> And this huge Castle, standing here sublime,
> I love to see the look with which it braves,
> Cased in the unfeeling armour of old time,
> The lightning, the fierce wind, and trampling waves.

> Farewell, farewell the heart that lives alone,
> Housed in a dream, at distance from the Kind!
> Such happiness, wherever it be known,
> Is to be pitied; for 'tis surely blind.
> But welcome fortitude, and patient cheer,
> And frequent sights of what is to be borne!
> Such sights, or worse, as are before me here.—
> Not without hope we suffer and we mourn.

The sight of Spring, too, with all her fresh, sunny beauties, suggests, by way of contrast even, human tragedy and suffering. He is saddened by her very blitheness, and a little poem on her birds of a thousand blended notes, her flowers and budding twigs, is haunted by the refrain "What man has made of man!" Similarly after his joy in a lovely morning following a stormy night—bright sun, singing birds, the air filled with the pleasant noise of waters, the grass bright with rain-drops, the hare running races in her mirth—after such joy, keen as he used to feel in childhood, he fell into despondency:

> There may come another day to me—
> Solitude, pain of heart, distress, and poverty,
> My whole life I have lived in pleasant thought,
> As if life's business were a summer mood;
> As if all needful things would come unsought
> To genial faith, still rich in genial good;
> But how can He expect that others should
> Build for him, sow for him, and at his call
> Love him, who for himself will take no heed at all?
> I thought of Chatterton, the marvellous Boy,
> The sleepless Soul that perished in his pride;
> Of Him who walked in glory and in joy
> Following his plough, along the mountain-side . . .
> We poets in our youth begin in gladness;
> But thereof come in the end despondency and madness.

The poem does not end on this note: the sight of the old leech-gatherer, and a talk with him, avail to give him once more a man's fortitude and cheerfulness.

In a more general way, he is at times almost in despair about England's evil state:—

> She is a fen
> Of stagnant waters.

Yet a stronger faith supervenes:—

> It is not to be thought of that the Flood
> Of British Freedom, which, to the open sea
> Of the world's praise, from dark antiquity
> Hath flowed, "with pomp of waters, unwithstood,"
> Roused though it be full often to a mood
> Which spurns the check of salutary bands,
> That this most famous Stream in bogs and sands
> Should perish; and to evil and to good
> Be lost for ever.   In our halls is hung
> Armoury of the invincible Knights of old:
> We must be free or die, who speak the tongue
> That Shakspeare spake; the faith and morals hold
> Which Milton held.—In everything we are sprung
> Of Earth's first blood, have titles manifold.

To his more despondent mood, again, a slowly sinking star, which passes below the rocky horizon only to rise again next night, suggests, in contrast, the futility of human effort.

> We struggle with our fate,
> While health, power, glory, from their height decline,
> Depressed; and then extinguished; and our state,
> In this, how different, lost Star, from thine,
> That no tomorrow shall our beams restore.

When this deep sense that "chains tie us down by land and sea," that "we are pressed by heavy laws," becomes intolerable, he changes his outlook and seeks relief and readjustment in the simple beauties of the wild life and natural incidents he loved so well.

> No check, no stay, this Streamlet fears;
> How merrily it goes!
> 'Twill murmur on a thousand years,
> And flow as now it flows. . . .
> The blackbird amid leafy trees,
> The lark above the hill,
> Let loose their carols when they please,
> Are quiet when they will.
> With Nature never do they wage
> A foolish strife; they see
> A happy youth, and their old age
> Is beautiful and free.

In winning his relief he looks, it is true, only on one aspect of nature, and he either does not see, or ignores, that other of "nature red in tooth and claw"; he ascribes to the birds the sort of outlook on life that he himself would fain have, if he were as they. But this, in the particular circumstances, is not unnatural.

The intensity of his interest in human nature and its tragedies may be gauged, even apart from his own writings of another kind, by this recoil. As one is wont, from work-a-day life and responsibilities, to turn for recreation to scenes and conditions where such responsibilities, if they exist at all, exist only in a minor degree, so he finds his release from bondage in the loneliness and quiet beauties of the country. He is, as he says,

> Well pleased to recognise
> In nature and the language of the sense,
> The anchor of my purest thoughts, the nurse,
> The guide, the guardian of my heart, and soul
> Of all my moral being. . . .
> [Nature] can so inform
> The mind that is within us, so impress
> With quietness and beauty, and so feed
> With lofty thoughts, that neither evil tongues,
> Rash judgments, nor the sneers of selfish men,
> Nor greetings where no kindness is, nor all
> The dreary intercourse of daily life,
> Shall e'er prevail against us, or disturb
> Our cheerful faith that all which we behold
> Is full of blessings.

In the contemplation of nature, then, serenity may be recovered. A more universal view of life and death and of our place in the greater scheme of things may be attained and fed

> 'Mid Nature's old felicities,
> Rocks, rivers, and smooth lakes more clear than glass
> Untouched, unbreathed upon.

Thus emancipated, then, Wordsworth can see that the two worlds the natural and the human, are really cognate and correspondent. Each has its place in the universal order of things; each is a vital part of the sum of things. If in

the common daisy he finds "some concord with humanity,"
so, too, an old palsied beggar is not without the pale of the
world's harmony.

> 'Tis Nature's law
> That none, the meanest of created things,
> Of forms created the most vile and brute,
> The dullest or most noxious, should exist
> Divorced from good—a spirit and pulse of good,
> A life and soul, to every mode of being
> Inseparably linked.

The world becomes to Wordsworth one great and closely
interconnected whole, and he comes to proclaim

> How exquisitely the individual Mind
> (And the progressive powers perhaps no less
> Of the whole species) to the external World
> Is fitted!—and how exquisitely, too—
> Theme this but little heard of among men—
> The external World is fitted to the Mind.

To Wordsworth, in his most exalted moments, a great vision
is laid open. In spite of the discords which he poignantly
recognises—the "solitary anguish," the "ill sights of
madding passions mutually inflamed"; in spite too of the
wreckage wrought by natural forces—he can yet catch the
deeper harmonies of a "music of the spheres." The whole
creation becomes a living, pulsing entity. Something of
this he gives in Tintern Abbey:—

> With an eye made quiet by the power
> Of harmony, and the deep power of joy,
> We see into the life of things. . . .
> And I have felt
> A presence that disturbs me with the joy
> Of elevated thoughts; a sense sublime
> Of something far more deeply interfused,
> Whose dwelling is the light of setting suns,
> And the round ocean and the living air,
> And the blue sky, and in the mind of man:
> A motion and a spirit, that impels
> All thinking things, all objects of all thought,
> And rolls through all things.

Lovely indeed was the apocalypse which he won from his

contemplations of lonely nature and of humanity.   Like
Goethe he realised how natural forces

> Bilden wüthend eine Kette
> Der tiefsten Wirkung rings umher.

On the other hand, he had deep recognitions

> Of Truth, of Grandeur, Beauty, Love, and Hope,
> And melancholy Fear subdued by Faith.

By his poet's insight he could, as Palgrave says, "identify
nature with the human heart more closely than the man who
either, from inferior imaginative power, does not feel the
inherent vitality in all things, or who regards them as
simple subjects for scientific investigation."

In conclusion, then, we may say that to Wordsworth, as
to other great poets or philosophers or men of science, past
and present, the essential unity of Nature and Humanity
seems to be in no small measure revealed.   The form in
which seers of this kind express their vision is various.
One will utter it in the form of far-reaching physical and
biological laws, another under the guise of mythological
creations, still another in the pantheistic view of a divine
power permeating and vitalising the whole universe.   So
the universe becomes a mighty heritage for man, twofold
yet inseparable: on the one hand Nature with her huge
forces, her complexities, and her amazing beauties; on the
other, Humanity with its lofty aspirations, its failures and
tragedies, and its ever-renewed will to emerge from the
shadows and to see "beyond the veil."   And to the question,
Is lonely nature a "proper study of mankind?" it must be
answered that if we humbler folk would also become "heirs
of the ages" we must reach an understanding not only of
inward thought and emotion, but also of the outword
world.   We must learn the secret whereby the one and the
other can be reconciled, not forgetting that in Wordsworth's
view at least it is Nature that chiefly contributes to the
knowledge of Humanity itself; for it is she that can teach us

> More of man,
> Of moral evil and of good,
> Than all the sages can.

Sir Thomas Browne[1]

In times like these one turns with a certain relief to the writings of men who, though living themselves in perilous days, yet in their books refer either not at all, or hardly at all, to the dangers through which they passed. As Professor Grierson pointed out, in his inaugural lecture at Edinburgh, the connection between literature and history is slight or indirect. Chaucer, he said, "had lived through the period of the French wars, but there was no allusion to them in his work." So, if we look for other examples, Shakespeare, if I remember rightly, has singularly few, if any, clear references to the troubles of his time. Then we have Sir Thomas Browne himself, who lived during the upheavals of the Civil War, yet tranquilly pursued his solitary studies and "retired imaginations"; who keenly desired the victory of the Royalists, yet daily discharged his professional duties as a doctor, and also carried on untiringly his researches in botany, in natural history and in antiquities. Henry Vaughan and Izaak Walton, two of Browne's contemporaries, are also, I believe, cases in point. Charles Lamb, who lived through the Napoleonic Wars, and who was a great admirer of Browne, was another instance. We have then varied and excellent authority for dismissing the preoccupations of history and turning for a time to the contentments of literature.

Before speaking of Sir Thomas Browne's books, let me recall to you very briefly the outlines of his uneventful life.

Born in 1605, in Cheapside, he lost his father, a merchant belonging to an old Cheshire family, very early; yet from his father, as Symonds gives reasonable cause for thinking, the son's later mysticism and strong religious feeling may well have been inherited. The boy was sent to Winchester School, and stayed there till he was 18. He then, in 1623,

[1] Read to the English Association (Newcastle Branch) in December, 1916.

went to Oxford, where he was "entered a gentleman commoner of Broadgate Hall," or, as it was soon to be called, Pembroke College. He became a Bachelor of Arts in June, 1626; and in due course proceeded Master of Arts. He then turned his attention to medicine, and is said by some (for instance, by Dr. Johnson) to have practised as a doctor in Oxfordshire. More probably, however, as Edmund Gosse points out, this episode belongs to a somewhat later period, viz. 1633 or 1634. It was possibly at the close of 1626 that he went to Ireland in company with his stepfather, Sir Thomas Dutton, and visited the forts and castles, which, owing to the breach with France, were attracting attention. When peace was restored, in 1630, Browne went to the Continent to pursue his medical studies. He worked for a time at Montpelier, where there was a celebrated school of botany, and then passed on to Padua where the clinical teaching was exceptionally good. He next made his way to Holland, and after studying chemistry at Leyden took his degree of Doctor of Medicine in that town. He probably returned to England in 1633. Before long—Gosse thinks about 1635—we find him in or near Halifax in Yorkshire; and it was there that he wrote *Religio Medici*, which work, however, was not published for another seven or eight years. In 1637 he was incorporated a doctor of physic at Oxford, and it was apparently in the same year that he settled permanently in Norwich. His practice there, as is recorded by Wood, became extensive and successful. In 1641, when he was 36 years old, he married Dorothy Mileham. She was a lady, says Whitefoot, a friend of Browne's, "of such symmetrical proportion to her worthy husband, both in the graces of her body and mind, that they seemed to come together by a kind of natural magnetism." They lived happily together for 41 years, and had several children—whether 10 or 6 does not seem clear. Johnson says 10, but Gosse hesitates; J. A. Symonds even puts them at 11. The eldest son Edward, born either in 1642 or 1644, travelled a good deal, and became a famous doctor. He was appointed physician to Charles II., who held him to be "as learned as any of the College, and as well-bred as any of the Court."

In 1642, the year in which the Civil War broke out, and in which was fought the battle of Edgehill, the first, and unauthorised, edition of the *Religio Medici* was published. As Johnson says, it at once "excited the attention of the public, by the novelty of paradoxes, the dignity of sentiment, the quick succession of images, the multitude of abstruse allusions, the subtlety of disquisition, and the strength of language." You remember the circumstances of its appearance—how it had been written seven or eight years before at Halifax, and had then been passed about from hand to hand in manuscript; how a defective copy reached a publisher who unscrupulously printed it; how the Earl of Dorset saw it and drew Sir Kenelm Digby's attention to it; how Digby, within 24 hours according to the tale, procured a copy, read it, and wrote 12,000 or 13,000 words of *Observations* upon it, which he addressed to the Earl; how Browne heard the news, and at once wrote to Digby, saying that the edition was imperfect, and surreptitiously produced, and asking him to suspend his judgment until the authorised edition, which in self-defence he was about to issue in a few weeks, should be available. Digby, however, either did not or could not now intervene, and his precipitate animadversions, as Johnson calls them, were quickly printed. Shortly afterwards, viz. in 1643, the authorised edition came out. The book quickly became famous. Merryweather turned it into Latin, the universal language, and got it printed in Holland. From his version it was translated into Italian, German, Dutch, and French.

In this manner Browne's first great book was published. The rest of his life was passed uneventfully in his busy professional work, in writing new books, in his antiquarian and scientific studies, in the collection of curiosities, and in intercourse and correspondence with his friends and family.

In 1646 he published the *Enquiries into Vulgar and Common Errors*, a work which, as Johnson says, "as it arose not from fancy and invention, but from observation and books, and contained not a single discourse of one continued tenor, of which the latter part arose from the former, and an enumeration of many unconnected particulars, must have

K

been the collection of years." In 1658, or perhaps, as Gosse thinks,[2] in the autumn of 1657, some ancient urns were discovered in Norfolk. The incident led Browne, early in 1658, to write his *Hydriotaphia, or Urn-Burial: a Discourse of Sepulchral Urns.* Let me quote Johnson again. "There is perhaps none of his works which better exemplifies his reading or memory. It is scarcely to be imagined, how many particulars he has amassed together, in a treatise which seems to have been occasionally written; and for which therefore no materials could have been previously collected." To this discourse was appended *The Garden of Cyrus, or the Quincuncial or Network Plantations of the Ancients.* Browne prettily explains the conjunction of a book on burial with one on gardens (or paradises) in the Epistle Dedicatory to Nicholas Bacon, saying that he issued them together "since the delightfull World comes after death, and Paradise succeeds the Grave. Since the verdant state of things is the Symbole of the Resurrection, and to flourish in the state of Glory, we must first be sown in corruption."

No more of Browne's writings were published during his lifetime. They were issued posthumously, at intervals. I will refer to them very briefly in one moment, in order to emphasise the singular variety—I had almost said the desultoriness—of his interests, and the wide range of his curiosity or learning. But let me first chronicle the remaining external events of his long life. In 1665, when he was 60 years old, he was made an honorary fellow of the College of Physicians, as a man *virtute et literis ornatissimus.* Six years later, in 1671, he received the honour of Knighthood on the occasion of a visit by Charles II. to Norwich. "Thus he lived," says Johnson, "in high reputation, till in his seventy-sixth year he was seized with a cholick, which. after having tortured him about a week, put an end to his life, at Norwich, on his birthday, October 19, 1682." His wife survived him three years. Browne's friend Whitefoot has left a full personal description of him, which I epitomise. As in name, so in complexion and hair, he was brown. He was of moderate height and of a comfortable habit of body. He wore plain but very warm clothing.

[2] Gosse (E.) Sir Thomas Browne (*English Men of Letters*), 1905.

He had a tenacious memory; he was always cheerful, but rarely jocose—and then blushed at his levity. He was parsimonious in nothing but his time. He disliked sloth and idleness, and would say "he could not do nothing." He was liberal in his house entertainments and in his charity; and he left a comfortable estate, though not a great one, to his wife and children.

As to his other writings: in 1684 *Certain Miscellany Tracts* were published. They dealt with such matters as *Plants mentioned in Scripture*; *The Fishes eaten by our Saviour with his Disciples after his Resurrection ; Hawks and Falconry ; Ropalic or Gradual Verses* (i.e. verses in which the first word contains one syllable, the second two, the third three, and so on. He mentions also many other curious methods of versifying). Other tracts are on *Languages, and particularly the Saxon Tongue ;* on *Artificial Hills, Mounts or Barrows ;* on *Apollo's Answers to Croesus, King of Lydia.* There is the *Musaeum Clausum*, too, in which he describes imaginary treasures, oddities and curiosities which it would have delighted his heart to possess—such as the skin of a snake bred out of the spinal marrow of a man; or a transcendent perfume made of the richest odorates of both the Indies, with this inscription: Deos rogato Totum ut te faciant, Fabulle, nasum (Pray the gods, Fabullus, to transform you into one big nose).[3]

In 1690 there appeared the *Letter to a Friend upon the occasion of the Death of his intimate Friend.* Pater, in his *Appreciations* speaks of it as a "unique morsel of literature"; and his characteristic criticism is that this "very singular letter," together with the *Hydriotaphia*, "is perhaps, after all, the best justification of Browne's literary reputation, as it were his own curiously figured urn, and treasure-place of immortal memory." In 1712 was published *Repertorium ; or, some Account of the Tombs and Monuments in the Cathedral Church of Norwich*; and a tract *Concerning some urns found in Brampton-Fields, in Norfolk.* In 1716 came *Christian Morals*, which was edited by Jeffery, archdeacon of Norwich, and published by the Cambridge University Press. Lastly there are *Notes on certain Birds*

[3] *Catullus*, 13.

and Fishes found in Norfolk, and shorter tracts on *The Ostrich*, on a *Thunder Storm in Norwich*, 1665, on *Dreams*, etc., etc.   Such, then, is a fairly complete list of Browne's literary labours.   It reveals the variety of his pursuits and of his learning, and his delight in the strange and unfamiliar things of nature and of human experience.

This short record of his life and of the publication of his books must suffice.   Let me now touch upon some of his writings separately, pointing out a few of their characteristics and giving some attention to their style.

The *Vulgar Errors* contains a great deal that is delightfully entertaining.   It is in fact typically "a quaint and curious volume of forgotten lore."   In it Browne treats of many old fancies and superstitions.   He discusses seriously, for instance, whether the badger has the legs on one side shorter than on the other, to enable it, presumably, to run easily on steeply sloping banks.   Most people had an idea that the legs on the left side were shorter; but Browne does not think that to have them shorter either on one side or the other is according to Reason.   He thinks that if any such monstrosity is to occur, it is more likely in the case of the cross-legs (one fore-leg and one hind-leg), since it is on these cross-legs that quadrupeds progress.   The chapter illustrates amusingly a rather risky method of nature-study; viz. by theorising instead of observing. Then he discusses the old idea that a bear brings forth her young in the form of a shapeless lump, to which she proceeds to give the right shape by licking it all over. Browne opposes this notion, and quotes two or three old authorities in support of his view.   Moreover, he thinks it is not according to the normal processes of nature, and concludes generally that the opinion is "repugnant both unto sense and Reason."   Elsewhere there is an entertaining chapter concerning weight.   In it he discusses the notion that men weigh heavier when dead than when alive.   He argues that it is unlikely; for although in the case of a man it is not easy actually to weigh the body just before death and immediately after, yet he has tried the experiment on chickens and on mice, and found no difference, dead or alive.   He goes on to say that if one feels a greater difficulty

in lifting a dead body it is probably due to the absence of
any responsive effort and aid in that body, and he compares
the trouble of lifting or supporting a person who is in a fit,
or who has fainted, or who is drunk. Again, he says that
many are " of opinion, and some learned men maintain, that
Men are lighter after meals than before." This also he
disbelieves, because he has weighed sundry persons of
different sex and ages. He concludes that the sense of
lightness is simply due to the personal feeling of vigour,
gained from the food taken, just as after a draught of wine a
man may seem lighter in himself although he be heavier
in the balance by the weight of the liquor he has swallowed.
In another place he discusses the Phoenix, that unique
bird "which after many hundred years burneth it self, and
from the ashes thereof ariseth up another." He quotes
various authorities for its existence, but concludes that
the evidence is not satisfactory. In still another place he
speaks of the idea that to see a hare crossing the highway
forbodes danger; that to meet a fox forebodes imposture;
that owls and ravens signify unlucky events; and that
the spilling of salt is of ill omen. He talks, too, of cracking
an egg-shell after the egg is eaten as a preventive of witchcraft; and of true lovers' knots, etc. He discusses in fact
innumerable odd by-ways of human history. The book,
however, from its lack of consecutiveness, and of any statement, or perhaps grasp, of general principles, is ill-adapted
for continuous reading, though it is excellent for dipping
into. As a dictionary of current misapprehensions and errors
it is incomplete; and for this reason Dr. Johnson rather
wished that Browne had not published it until towards
the close of his remaining 36 years of observation and study.
Historically it has the interest of revealing many of the
beliefs and credulities both of Browne himself and of his
contemporaries; scientifically, one often finds that Browne's
opinions are of small value. This inadequacy appears not
only in the *Vulgar Errors,* but elsewhere also. He held, for
instance, that the earth was stationary, and could not possibly
move; he believed in witchcraft; and he was persuaded that
it was possible to restore a flower to its first beauty after
it had been burnt to ashes. Well, in some respects, Browne

was behind his own times; and one remembers that the Royal Society, constituted in 1662, did not admit him to its Fellowship, though that was an honour which Browne seems to have coveted, and to which, through his acquaintance with scientific men. and his reputation, he probably thought himself entitled. They however perhaps regarded him rather as a curiosity-hunter and a visionary than as a trustworthy scientist with a firm grip of the general laws of nature.

The MS. of his book on *Christian Morals* was read by one of his daughters at the time he wrote it, which seems to have been during the last years of his life. Shortly after his death it got mislaid among other papers, and was not discovered for over 30 years. Then, in 1716, it was promptly published. It consists of 60 or 70 octavo pages of sermonettes on the conduct of life. Here is one of them (I., 15):--

"Let not the sun in Capricorn [i.e. even when the days are shortest] go down upon thy wrath, but write thy wrongs in Ashes. Draw the Curtain of night upon injuries, shut them up in the Tower of Oblivion [i.e. a Tower of imprisonment among the Persians: whoever was put therein was as it were buried alive, and it was death for any but to name him] and let them be as though they had not been. To forgive our Enemies, yet hope that God would punish them, is not to forgive enough. To forgive them ourselves and not to pray God to forgive them, is a partial piece of Charity. Forgive thine enemies totally, and without any reserve that however God will revenge thee."

The whole book contains much that is interesting and characteristic, and it is, as J. A. Symonds[4] says, "massy with condensed wisdom." It is sententious, but picturesque, and its broad truths are tellingly phrased. From it a small Book of Proverbs might almost be compiled. Listen to these, for example: "Let Age not Envy draw wrinkles in thy cheeks" (I. 13); "Annihilate not the Mercies of God by the Oblivion of Ingratitude" (I. 21); "Good admonitions Knock not always in vain" (II. 6); "The Race of Delight

---

[4] In his introduction to *Religio Medici*, etc. (Walter Scott, 1886).

is short, and Pleasures have mutable faces" (II. 1). This
last one, by the way, contains an entire hexameter:—
"[The] Race of Delight is short, and Pleasures have mutable
faces." We shall observe other examples of such lapses
elsewhere. Browne's love of alliteration, assonance and
antithesis is also very manifest. For example: "To strenu-
ous Minds there is an inquietude in overquietness, and no
laboriousness in labour" (I. 33); "Festination may prove
Precipitation; Deliberating delay may be wise cunctation,
and slowness no sloathfulness" (I. 33); "Let Anger walk
hanging down the head; Let Malice go manacled, and Envy
fetter'd after thee" (I. 2); "They do most by Books, who
could do much without them" (II. 4). There are many
examples, too, of his ready rhetoric and happy allusiveness.
This, for instance: "In this virtuous Voyage of thy Life
hall not about like the Ark, without the use of Rudder,
Mast, or Sail, and bound for no Port. Let not Disappointment cause Despondency, nor difficulty despair. Think
not that you are Sailing from *Lima* to *Manillia*, when you
may fasten up the Rudder, and sleep before the Wind:
but expect rough Seas, Flaws, and contrary Blasts: and
'tis well, if by many cross Tacks and Veerings you arrive
at the Port" (I. 1). Or this again, "Become not thine
own Parasite. Be deaf unto thy self, and be not betrayed
at home. Self-credulity, pride, and levity lead unto self-
Idolatry. There is no *Damocles* like unto self opinion, nor
any *Siren* to our own fawning Conceptions. To magnify
our minor things, or hug ourselves in our apparitions; to
afford a credulous Ear unto the clawing suggestions of
fancy; to pass our days in painted mistakes of our selves
. . . are blandishments of self love, worse than outward
delusion" (I. 23). Or once more: "Be not a *Hercules
furens* abroad, and a Poltron within thy self. . . . To well
manage our Affections, and wild Horses of *Plato*, are the
highest Circenses; and the noblest Digladiation is in the
Theater of our selves; for therein our inward Antagonists,
not only like common Gladiators, with ordinary weapons
and down right Blows make at us, but also like Retiary
and Laqueary Combatants, with Nets, Frauds, and En-
tanglements, fall upon us. Weapons for such combats

are not to be forged at *Lipara* : *Vulcan's* Art doth nothing in this internal Militia : wherein not the Armour of *Achilles*, but the Armature of *St. Paul*, gives the Glorious day, and Triumphs not Leading up into Capitols, but up into the highest Heavens" (I. 24).

Here also are two picturesque sentences: "Too many there be to whom a Dead Enemy smells well, and who find Musk and Amber in Revenge" (III. 12); and again, "If thou must needs have Revenge of thine Enemy, with a soft tongue break his Bones, heap Coals of Fire on his Head, forgive him, and enjoy it" (III. 12). It sounds like a rather ghoulish sort of forgiveness!

Now and again his manner recalls Marcus Aurelius, as in this: "Though the World be Histrionical, and most Men live Ironically, yet *be thou what thou singly art, and personate only thy self. Swim smoothly in the stream of thy Nature, and live but one Man*" (III. 20).

As to single phrases—"Jewels five words long"—they of course abound. Several you will have noticed already, such as *The Oblivion of Ingratitude*. Elsewhere (III. 6) speaking of those who persist in iniquity, he says they become *Deaf unto the Thunder of the Laws*. On the other hand those who "cultivate the good seeds which nature hath set in them, prove not shrubs but *Cedars in their Generation*" (I. 9). *The Oblivion of Ingratitude, The Thunder of the Laws, Cedars in their Generation*—assuredly preachers seeking titles for their sermons, or novelists for their novels, might do worse than turn the pages of Sir Thomas Browne.

It is not unnatural that, in such a collection as this of wise saws and precepts—the harvest of his experience—there should be echoes, even exact reduplications, of what he had written in earlier books. The last sentence I quoted, for example, containing the phrase "not shrubs but Cedars in their Generation," is almost word for word as it appears in the *Letter to a Friend*. I have noticed other instances both as regards the *Letter to a Friend*, and *Religio Medici*. In *Religio Medici* you may remember this: "Though I think no man can live well once, but he that could live twice, yet for my own part I would not live over my hours past, or begin again the thread of my days: not upon

Cicero's ground, because I have lived them well, but for fear I should live them worse." That is tersely and admirably put. It is not bettered, I think, in the older man's version (in *Christian Morals*, III. 25). But I must not linger over these echoes of his past writings. Let me, in leaving the *Christian Morals*, read you a few lines from the third part. They reveal something of the theory and practice of Browne's own life. "Desert not thy title to a Divine particle and union with invisibles. Let true Knowledge and Virtue tell the lower World thou art a part of the higher. Let thy Thoughts be of things which have not entred into the Hearts of Beasts: Think of things long past and long to come; acquaint thy self with the Choragium of the Stars, and consider the vast expansion beyond them. Let Intellectual Tubes give thee a glance of things, which visive Organs reach not. Have a glimpse of incomprehensibles, and Thoughts of things, which Thoughts but tenderly touch. Lodge immaterials in thy Head: ascend unto invisibles: fill thy Spirit with Spirituals, with the mysteries of Faith, the magnalities of Religion, and thy Life with Honour of God."

The *Garden of Cyrus, or the Quincunx*, to which I now ask you to turn, is again a work in which many of Browne's characteristics are to be found. We find style that is melodious and rhythmical, and we find style of a note-book baldness. His Latinism, or as Coleridge calls it, his Hyperlatinism, is also apparent, as one extraordinary specimen which I shall recall to you will show. We see his poetical, if fantastic, imagination; and we see his desultoriness, his brooding mysticism, and his jottings about botanical curiosities. Browne in this book regards the number Five as permeating much both of nature and of art. His

"poet's eye, in a fine frenzy rolling,
Doth glance from heaven to earth, from earth to heaven."

and everywhere discovers Five, in the form of a quincunx. He accepts Four however (e.g. in the four corners of a square, rhombus, or parallelogram) as often equivalent to Five, since if we join the points where the lines containing opposite angles meet, the point of intersection is the latent 5th

point.   Similarly he accepts Three (as in the points of a **V**),
. . .   since by producing the lines into an **X** the
5 points are again secured.   Nor is Nine
. . .   intractable; for Five was in old days, he says,
"surnamed the number of justice, as justly
. . .   dividing between the digits, and hanging in
the centre of Nine, described by square
numeration, which angularly divided will make the de-
cussated number."[5]   To decussate, by the way, is briefly
defined by Webster as "to cut or divide in the form of **X**";
which letter Browne describes as "the Emphatical decussation, or fundamental figure."   In it we get the five
essential points : 2 at the top, one in the middle, 2 at
the bottom.   As this was a favourite form for planting
trees, so also it is the basis of network.   To take things,
however, in their order: Browne begins with the Garden
of Eden.   After touching on its situation, he mentions
the Hanging Gardens of Babylon, and so comes to the
Persians and to Cyrus, "the first man whom we actually know
to have planted a quincunx."[6]   Browne refers to Xenophon,
and proceeds, "all stories do look upon Cyrus, as the splendid
and regular planter."   By him the rows and orders of the
trees were "so handsomely disposed: or five trees so set
together, that a regular angularity, and through prospect
was left on every side."   Other instances of the ancient
use of this figure are given; which figure, Browne says,
"he that more nearly considereth, in the form of its square
Rhombus, and Decussation, with the several commodities,
mysteries, parallelismes, and resemblances, both in Art and
Nature, shall easily discern the elegancy of this order."
One of the examples he gives is the Garden of Eden, in which,
since "the tree of knowledge was placed in the middle . . .
whatever was the ambient figure; there wanted not a
centre and rule of decussation."   Other instances are the
beds of the ancients which were corded obliquely, "after the
manner of network"; their cross-legged seats; chess-boards;
nutcrackers and forceps.   In his description of these last,

[5] Chapter V.

[6] *S. Johnson's Works*, Vol. 12, p. 272.   *Lives of Sundry Eminent Persons.*
(Hansard, 1816.)

we get the *tour-de-force* of hyperlatinism which I mentioned.
"Mechanicks," he says, make use of the quincunx "for
forcipal Organs, and Instruments of incision; wherein
who can but magnifie the power of decussation, inservient to
contrary ends, solution and consolidation, union, and
division, illustrable from *Aristotle* in the old *Nucifragium*
or Nutcracker, and the Instruments of Evulsion, compression
or incision; which consisting of two *Vectes* or armes, con-
verted towards each other, the innitency and stresse being
made upon the hypomochlion or fulciment in the decussation,
the greater compression is made by the union of two im-
pulsors." This hyperlatinism, indeed, reminds one of a
passage in the Introduction to *Vulgar Errors*, a work which
he had at first thought of writing in Latin. But he changed
his mind, although, as he says, "the quality of the Subject
will sometimes carry us into expressions beyond meer
English apprehensions. And indeed, if elegancy still
proceedeth, and English Pens maintain that stream, we
have of late observed to flow from many; we shall within
few years be fain to learn Latine to understand English,
and a work will prove of equal facility in either." But let
that pass. Other illustrations of the quincunx he draws
from the arrangement of the cohorts and maniples in the
Roman legion; from the form of cities (Babylon was square,
Nineveh of "a longilaterall figure"); from the shape of
Moses' Tables of the Law (which were oblong). Turning to
botany, he finds that many leaves "are overwrought with
Net-work elegantly containing this order, which plainly
declareth the naturality of this texture; and how the
needle of nature delighteth to work, even in low and doubtful
vegetations." Then come zoological instances, from the
network in the skins of certain snakes, birds, fishes, etc.
Even the locomotion of animals, he says, is made "with
analogy unto this figure . . . and as the station of most
Quadrupeds is made upon a long square, so in their motion
they make a Rhomboides; their common progression being
performed Diametrally, by decussation and cross ad-
vancement of their legges." After some further analogies
we have several pages of irrelevant queries and botanical
oddities, till he comes back to the quincunx latent in the

cylindrical figure of trees. He turns aside then to colours
and shadows and darkness and light; and here we get, in his
more mystical vein, this well-known passage: "Light that
makes things seen, makes some things invisible, were it not
for darkness and the shadow of the earth, the noblest
part of the Creation had remained unseen, and the Stars
in heaven as invisible as on the fourth day, when they were
created above the Horizon, with the Sun, or there was not
an eye to behold them. The greatest mystery of Religion
is expressed by adumbration, and in the noblest part of
Jewish Types, we finde the Cherubims shadowing the Mercy-
seat. Life it self is but the shadow of death, and souls
departed but the shadows of the living: All things fall under
this name. The Sunne it self is but the dark simulachrum,
and light but the shadow of God." Browne next applies
his quincunxes to the physiology of sight, and to intellectual
perceptions; and so we get on to Egyptian and Platonic
mysticism. Lastly, after mentioning the quintuple section
of the cone (into ellipse, parabola, hyperbola, circle and
triangle) he comes to the "conjugall or Wedding Number"
and other mysteries and mystical problems. Then the
book concludes with the famous passage beginning "But
the Quincunx of Heaven runs low, and 'tis time to close
the five ports of Knowledge"—a passage to which I shall
refer again in speaking of Coleridge's criticism of Browne.

That Browne in this essay recognises how devious his
course may seem to readers is clear from the Preface. He
writes as follows: "That in this Garden Discourse, we range
into extraneous things, and many parts of Art and Nature,
we follow herein the example of old and new Plantations,
wherein noble spirits contented not themselves with Trees,
but by the attendance of Aviaries, Fish-Ponds, and all
variety of Animals, they made their gardens the Epitome
of the earth." The further question, how far this essay is a
tour-de-force rather than an expression of Browne's definite
conviction, may be judged by comparing with it a passage
from the *Vulgar Errors*. He is speaking (in Book IV.,
chapter 12) of the Great Climacterical Year, that is 63;
and, from considering the component numbers of 63 (7 and
9) he is led to mention the notions of secret virtues in other

numbers, for instance 1, 3, 4, 6, 10: so that, as he says, "not only 7 and 9, but all the rest have had their Elogies [eulogies] . . . every one extolling number, according to his subject, and as it advantaged the present discourse in hand."[7] Yet if Browne, in reducing things to his quincunx reveals himself as a whimsical Procrustes, he shows no less that he is a poet and a mystic; and as Symonds says, "that aura, or spiritual afflatus of divine mystery, which permeated his imagination, tempted him to follow such lines of enquiry."

With regard to that little work called *A Letter to a Friend*, let me read a few lines from Pater's Appreciation of Sir Thomas Browne. Browne, says Pater, "is writing in a very complex situation—to a friend, upon occasion of the death of a common friend. The deceased apparently had been little known to Browne himself till his recent visits, while the intimate friend to whom he is writing had been absent at the time; and the leading motive of Browne's letter is the deep impression he has received during those visits, of a sort of physical beauty in the coming of death, with which he still surprises and moves his reader. There had been, in this case, a tardiness and reluctancy in the circumstances of dissolution, which had permitted him, in the character of a physician, as it were to assist at the spiritualising of the bodily frame by natural process; a wonderful new type of a kind of mortified grace being evolved by the way. The spiritual body had anticipated the formal moment of death; the alert soul, in that tardy decay, changing its vesture gradually, and as if piece by piece." To Pater's description, however, of "this elfin letter" as he calls it, perhaps a brief reminder may be added. The letter is not so homogeneous and direct as one might conclude. Browne writes here also with many digressions and excursions concerning incidental matters; and Johnson's general comment on Browne's style of composition is one that recurs to the mind. He says that Browne's "exuberance of knowledge, and plenitude of ideas, sometimes obstruct the tendency of his reasoning and the clearness

[7] *Works of Sir T. Browne*: Sayle's edition, Vol. II., p. 162. (Grant, 1912.)

of his decisions: on whatever subject he employed his mind, there started up immediately so many images before him, that he lost one by grasping another. His memory supplied him with so many illustrations, parallel or dependent notions, that he was always starting into collateral considerations: but the spirit and vigour of his pursuit always gives delight; and the reader follows him, without reluctance, through his mazes, in themselves flowery and pleasing, and ending at the point originally in view" (pp. 288–9). So in this letter Browne is beguiled into topics that are little to the point, and towards the end gives his correspondent a homily of seven pages on living virtuously.[8] He does conclude however with what is doubtless a last reference to that tranquil merging of this life into the next which is the keynote of the little book. "Since there is something in us," he says, "that must still live on, join both Lives together; unite them in thy thoughts and Actions, and live in one but for the other. He who thus ordereth the Purposes of this Life, will never be far from the next, and is in some measure already in it, by an happy Conformity, and close Apprehension of it."

I mentioned, in connection with the *Christian Morals*, one or two of the notable phrases that occur in this *Letter to a Friend*. Let me, before leaving the subject, recall to you two or three other phrases and descriptive sentences. Of the dead he speaks as "that dark Society." A body pined and attenuated by sickness he calls, with realistic quaintness, "a light Bit for the Grave." Of his patient's outlook on life and its reputed felicities he says: "His sober Contempt of the World wrought no *Democritism* or *Cynicism*, no laughing or snarling at it." He describes the change in sleep and dreams of the patient thus: "He was now past the healthful Dreams of the Sun, Moon and Stars, in their Clarity and proper Courses. 'Twas too late to dream of Flying, of Limpid Fountains, smooth Waters, white Vestments, and fruitful green Trees, which are the Visions of healthful Sleeps, and at good Distance from the Grave."

[8] These pages, Symonds suggests, were intended as a sort of introduction to *Christian Morals*, the *Letter* having been at first printed as a prelude to that work.

It recalls, doesn't it (?) the tranquillity of Wordsworth's sonnet to *Sleep* :

> . . . " the fall of rivers, winds and seas,
> Smooth fields, white sheets of water, and pure sky."

His description is good, again, of those who, though well on in years, are yet unwilling to die: "Many, tho' old, often stick fast unto the World, and seem to be drawn like Cacus's Oxen, backward, with great Struggling and Reluctancy unto the Grave." Lastly, this about covetousness is also excellent: "Covetousness," he says, "makes our own Death sweet unto others, bitter unto our selves; gives a dry Funeral, Scenical Mourning, and no wet Eyes at the Grave."

But let us turn to the *Religio Medici*. As it is one of Browne's best known works, there is the less need to linger much over it. It is mainly occupied with religious meditations; with musings on man's life, death and immortality. It dwells on God's eternity; on the mysteries of faith (in which Browne "loves to lose himself"); on the ways of God concerning man and the universe, as He works now through Nature—"that streight and regular line," as Browne calls it, meaning the direct, normal operations of the laws of nature—now through Fortune, which Browne calls "that serpentine and crooked line," meaning those indirect and unexpected methods which God sometimes uses to accomplish His designs. It tells us, in fact, with some confidence, a good deal about God; it also tells us something about guardian spirits and angels, about devils, about man the microcosm. It treats too of man's virtues (and notably of charity), and of man's sins; his punishment and his salvation. We learn, moreover, as is natural in an auto-biographical work, a great deal about the author himself— his temperament and tastes. What are the characteristics that chiefly emerge? Perhaps we are first struck by his varied learning, his intellectual curiosity, his mystical imagination, his genius of expression. Then we recall his cheerful piety, his tolerant breadth of view, his human helpfulness. The work is admittedly, as a system of religious philosophy, of minor importance: its desultoriness, and its lack of constructive development, put such a claim out of the question. As Pater says, for instance, Browne's "contributions to 'evidence' . . . hardly tell, because he writes out of view of a really philosophical criticism. What does tell in him, in this direction, is the witness he brings to men's instinct of survival—the 'intimations of immortality,' as Wordsworth terms them, which were natural with him in surprising force." As literature, however, it contains much that is great, much that is of perennial value. Many things in it are admirably said: we delight at one time in his homely yet effective words, at another in his deliberate periods and stately progress; we are astonished at the swift turns of phrase whereby he will open up an unsuspected vista, a noble perspective; sometimes, too, we are fascinated by the cadence of his sentences, compact of melody and of haunting rhythmic beauty; though at other times, it must be admitted, his composition is poor, and he has false prose-rhythms.

One or two of these points may be illustrated. That his use of homely expressions is not uncommon in other books, we have already seen. Here are one or two more from the *Religio Medici*. "My conscience," he says, "will not *give me the lye*, if I say" so and so. Again, being of sound bodily health, he can call himself, he says, if he dies, "as *wholesome a morsel for the worms as any*." Once more, "Heads that are disposed unto Schism . . . do subdivide *and mince themselves almost into Atoms*." Lastly, there are Christians, he says, who "disdain to *suck Divinity from the flowers* of Nature." Let me next illustrate what I said about the phrases by which he suddenly lifts our point of view from a lower plane to a higher, so that we see the ordinary incidents of life in a new and greater perspective. In one place he is speaking about diseases, and their final cure by death, which, he says, "though nauseous to queasie stomachs, yet to prepared appetites is Nectar, and a pleasant potion of immortality." In half a sentence he swings up from "queasie stomachs" to Eternity. Again, he says, "I cannot relate the History of my life, the occurrences of my days, the escapes of dangers, and hits of chance, with a *Bezo las Manos* to Fortune, or a bare *Gramercy* to my good Stars": his gratitude is due, he explains, to the watchful

providence of God himself. "A bare *Gramercy* to my
good Stars" is a pretty transition from the immediate
bustle of life to a serene and high view of it. Similarly he
says, "If to be born under *Mercury* disposeth us to be
witty, under *Jupiter* to be wealthy; I do not owe a Knee
unto these, but unto that merciful Hand that hath ordered
my indifferent and uncertain nativity unto such benevolous
Aspects." He transfers the attention from man's wealth
and wit first to the planets and their influence, and then to
an all-embracing Power. In another place he is explaining
that he does not greatly esteem relics of the saints (such
as the ashes of John the Baptist, or nails from the Cross).
One reason for his attitude is, he says, "the slender and
doubtful respect I have always held unto Antiquities.
For that indeed which I admire, is far before Antiquity,
that is Eternity; and that is, God himself." Another
example which you may recall is the passage in which he
tells us he is "naturally amorous of all that is beautiful,"
so that as he says, "I can look a whole day upon a handsome picture, though it be but of an Horse." You will
remember how he rises from the handsome picture of an
Horse to the general beauty and harmony of the world and
to "the music of the Sphears"; and in like manner from
vulgar "Tavern-Musick" to the "harmony which intel-
lectually sounds in the ears of God." Perhaps these instances will serve to remind you how often Browne, in his
transcendent or soaring fashion, relates little things to great
principles; how he "hitches his wagon to a star."

To some of the more technical features of Sir Thomas
Browne's rhythms I shall come shortly. Let me say here
that while in many places his style is strangely beautiful,
in others (both in the *Religio* and in the *Urn-Burial*) it is
far from admirable. And first, as a very perfect specimen
of English prose, let me quote this one passage, in which
we get Browne's vision of the Last Day and of the final
justice. I shall speak of it again later. "This is the day
that must make good that great attribute of God, His
justice; that must reconcile those unanswerable doubts
that torment the wisest understandings; and reduce those
seeming inequalities and respective distributions in this

'L

world, to an equality and recompensive Justice in the next. This is that one day, that shall include and comprehend all that went before it, wherein, as in the last scene, all the Actors must enter, to compleat and make up the Catastrophe of this great piece. This is the day whose memory hath onely power to make us honest in the dark, and to be vertuous without a witness." Elsewhere, however, there are flies in the amber. For one thing, both punctuation and syntax have been deplored—e.g. by Coleridge and Pater. Here and there, too, his prose runs into irritating verse-rhythms. For example, in one place we get two consecutive blank verses:

> Those vulgar Heads that rudely stare about
> And with a gross rusticity admire
> His works.

Elsewhere he ends a sentence with the closing half of a hexameter, "one in the Trunk of a Cedar"—which, from its position before a full stop, is the more noticeable. The Dedication to the *Urn-Burial*, again, gives further instances, such as these two complete hexameters:

> Who knows the fate of his bones, or how often he is to be
>   buried;

and this:

> Daily command the view of so many imperial faces.

In such false rhythms, however, Browne at least sins in good company. As he says in one place, in the *Religio*, when speaking of harmony and music, "all are naturally inclined unto Rhythme. This made Tacitus, in the very first line of his Story,[9] fall upon a verse; and Cicero, the worst of Poets, but declaiming for a Poet,[10] falls in the very first sentence upon a perfect Hexameter."

It is time, however, to turn to the *Urn-Burial*. This was published, you remember, in 1658, the urns themselves having been found near the end of 1657. Pater's reference to the matter is not easy to understand. He says that Browne "had drawn up a short account of the circumstance

---

[9] *Annals*, I. 1. "Urbem Romam a principio reges habuere."

[10] *Pro Archia*, I. 1. ". . . exercitatio dicendi, *in qua me non infitior mediocriter esse* versatum."

at the moment; but it was after ten years' brooding that he put forth the finished treatise." That would throw back the discovery of the urns to 1647 or 1648; for which date he gives no authority. The find consisted of 40 or 50 urns, dug up in a field at Old Walsingham. These urns, containing human bones and ashes, Browne believed to be Roman, judging not from archaeological knowledge but from the fact that they were found near a Roman garrison. In this belief he was in error. Gosse explains that, "as Sir John Evans has pointed out, the modern antiquary has only to glance at the frontispiece . . . to see that the vessels were not of Roman but of Saxon origin." The mistake is of course unfortunate. But though the foundation stone is thus knocked away, the marvellous structure still stands unshaken. Gosse continues that "we do not go to Browne to-day for antiquarian information—although some of his notes about coins are said to preserve their value."

The book is dedicated to Thomas Le Gros, a collector of ancient coins and other rarities; and if I wanted to epitomise its contents, I think I should take a single sentence from this dedication—"Who hath the oracle of his ashes, or whether they are to be scattered?" Browne begins by touching on the chief methods of disposing of dead bodies: ordinary burial in the earth, burning, destruction in the sea by fishes, destruction in the open air by birds and beasts. He reviews the burial customs and ceremonies of various races, and mentions different kinds of urns, coffins and sepulchres. He speaks also of their decoration, and of the substances found in them—oil, wine, rings, coins, chalices Urns and tombs have often been robbed, either for the sake of their wealth, or for the purposes of witchcraft, since "bones, hairs, nails, and teeth of the dead, were the treasures of old sorcerers." He then refers to the effect of fire in reducing the weight of bodies to a few pounds, in preserving them from putrefaction, and from profanation. After turning again to funeral rites and ceremonies, he is led to man's conception of a future state and to his belief in immortality. In this world, however, the quest for lasting fame and remembrance is a vain one. Monuments suffer destruction, "gravestones tell truth scarce forty years."

"To be read by bare inscriptions . . . and have new names given us like many of the mummies, are cold consolations unto the students of perpetuity." But "the sufficiency of Christian immortality . . . makes a folly of posthumous memory." "To subsist in lasting monuments . . . was large satisfaction unto old expectations. . . . But all this is nothing in the metaphysicks of true belief."

In this brief outline of the *Hydriotaphia*, then, we see once more how Browne passes from urns and bones, from things which are transitory and visible, up to those which are invisible and eternal.

As regards style, the book exhibits both the defects and the glories of Sir Thomas Browne. Sometimes we find sentences which have no main verb, and which are in fact mere note-book jottings. Or it may be that the subject is missing, as in this sentence—a sentence by the way which forms a complete paragraph, and which contains 94 words.

Nor in their cohabitation with Egyptians, crept into a custom of their exact embalming, wherein deeply slashing the muscles, and taking out the brains and entrails, they had broken the subject of so entire a resurrection, nor fully answered the types of Enoch, Elijah, or Jonah, which yet to prevent or restore, was of equal facility unto that rising power, able to break the fasciations and bands of death, to get clear out of the cerecloth, and an hundred pounds of ointment, and out of the sepulchre before the stone was rolled from it.

As I say, the subject is missing. It is really *The Jewish nation*, but to find it we must rummage in a previous paragraph. The long sentence trails on with merely commas for its punctuation. Well, isn't there a proverb which says something quite satisfactory about *easy writing* and *hard reading*?

So much for these defects. We may regard them as the shadows which throw into vivid relief such lovely and inspired passages as the two which I shall now quote, and to which I shall return later. Here is the first:

"There is no antidote against the opium of time which temporally considereth all things: our fathers find their graves in our short memories, and sadly tell us how we may be buried in our survivers. Gravestones tell truth scarce forty years. Generations pass while some trees stand, and old families last not three oaks. To be read by bare inscriptions like many in Gruter, to hope for eternity by enigmatical epithets or first letters of our names, to be studied by antiquaries, who we were, and have new names given us like many of the mummies are cold consolations unto the students of perpetuity, even by everlasting languages."

Secondly, let me take the first few lines of Chapter V. They are frequently quoted, but perhaps you will welcome them on that account with the greater pleasure:

" Now since these dead bones have already outlasted the living ones of Methuselah, and in a yard under ground, and thin walls of clay, outworn all the strong and specious buildings above it, and quietly rested under the drums and tramplings of three conquests ; what prince can promise such diuturnity unto his relicks, or might not gladly say,

> Sic ego componi versus in ossa velim?[11]

Time, which antiquates antiquities and hath an art to make dust of all things, hath yet spared these minor monuments."

As Symonds well says, the language is "sustained on a majestic note of eloquence." He comments on some of the rarer qualities of the style, "here displayed in rich maturity and heavy-scented blossom," and directs attention, in a way that recalls De Quincey, "to the unique feeling for verbal tone, for what may be called the musical colour of words, for crumbling cadences and the reverberation of stationary sounds in cavernous recesses."

In a survey of Browne's work, some little discussion of his prose rhythm is appropriate. To deal with its technical aspects in any full detail is of course impossible in the time at our disposal. Long passages would have to be examined and scanned; and the results, if we desired to offer more than tentative suggestions, would have to be tabulated and compared. Professor Saintsbury in his

---

[11] So may I lie when turned to dust.

History of English Prose Rhythm, gives selections from Browne covering a good many pages; but unfortunately he does not summarise matters. The vagueness, indeed, in which he leaves his readers concerning all the authors he examines, has been regretted by Mr. A. C. Clark, who, while praising many qualities in the book, is disappointed that the final judgment reached is only this: that "as the essence of verse-matter is its identity, at least in equivalence and recurrence, so the essence of prose-rhythm lies in variety and divergence." Is it possible to reach results that are in any degree more definite, at least as regards Browne? What Saintsbury does, you remember, is this. He selects a number of passages in which Browne's style is at its very best. Some of these he merely quotes; in others he indicates, by a vertical line, how the metrical feet are divided; in still others he gives each foot its detailed scansion, marking a stressed syllable long, and an unstressed syllable short. This traditional notation, though presenting, in a language like English, certain difficulties, works out intelligibly enough, and for comparative purposes has its advantages. Saintsbury, as I say, quotes only from Browne's finest passages. Perhaps for the object we have in view it will be better if we take first of all one or two specimens of Browne when he is *not* at his best—when his rhythm, in fact, is bad—and then compare these with an example or so of the lovely work he produces when at his highest level. I fancy we shall see that, as he emerges from a bald style to a beautiful style, certain feet in his rhythm recur more and more frequently. In order that we may be quite clear in what we are doing, perhaps I may recall to you one or two facts about rhythm and verses. Goodwin's *Greek Grammar* (p. 312 *seq.*) puts the matter lucidly, and with some omissions, etc., will serve as a basis.

The unit of measure is the short syllable (‿), which has the value of an ⅛ note or ♪ in music. This is called a *time* or *mora*. The long syllable (—) has twice the length of a short one, and has the value of a ¼ note or ♩ in music. It is the equivalent of, or is resolvable into, two short ones.

Feet are distinguished according to the number of *times* which they contain. The most common feet are the following:—

Feet of 3 times (in ⅜ time).

Trochee	— ◡	
Iambus	◡ —	
Tribrach	◡ ◡ ◡	

Feet of 4 times (in 2/4 time = 4/8 time).

Dactyl	— ◡ ◡
Anapaest	◡ ◡ —
Spondee	— —

Feet of 5 times (in 5/8 time).

Cretic	— ◡ —
Paeon primus	— ◡ ◡ ◡
Paeon quartus	◡ ◡ ◡ —
Bacchius	◡ — —
Antibacchius	— — ◡

Feet of 6 times (in 3/4 time = 6/8 time).

Ionic *a majore*	— — ◡ ◡
Ionic *a minore*	◡ ◡ — —
Choriambus	— ◡ ◡ —
Molossus	— — —
Ditrochee	— ◡ — ◡
Diiambus	◡ — ◡ —

Beyond these there are still longer feet (viz. of 7 or 8 times).

A verse is sometimes introduced by an incomplete foot of one or two syllables, like the upward or introductory beat in music. A long syllable may in certain cases be *shortened* so as to take the place of a short syllable. It is called irrational, and is marked >.[12]

So much, then, by way of introduction to the passages we are to consider. The clauses or phrases into which sentences fall I have, for convenience, shown separately, giving to each what, as it seems to me, may be regarded as its metrical division and scansion.

Let us take as our first example this piece, in which you will notice the bad punctuation and syntax, the monotonous similarity in the length of the clauses, the fidgety anapaestic or iambic lilt, and the incongruous introduction (especially in lines 5 and 12) of alien rhythms. It is from the *Urn-Burial* (p. 136, Dent's edition).

---

[12] On the other hand, I have here and there represented by < a short, or rather a short and a pause, having the value of a long.

1. That these were the urns of Romans   ‿ — | ‿ ‿ — | ‿ — | ‿

*2. from the common custom and place where they were found,   ‿ ‿ — | ‿ — | ‿ ‿ — | ‿ — | ‿ —

*3. is no obscure conjecture,   ‿ — | ‿ — | ‿ — | —

*4. not far from a Roman garrison   — — | ‿ ‿ — | ‿ — | ‿ <

5. and but five miles from Brancaster,   ‿ ‿ — — | ‿ — — | ‿

*6. set down by ancient record   > — | ‿ — | ‿ — | —

7. under the name of Brannodunum.   ‿ ‿ ‿ — | ‿ — | ‿ — | ‿

*8. And where the adjoining town,   ‿ — | ‿ ‿ — | ‿ —

9. containing seven parishes,   ‿ — | ‿ — | ‿ — | ‿ —

*10. in no very different sound,   ‿ — | ‿ ‿ — | ‿ ‿ —

11. but Saxon termination,   ‿ — | ‿ — | ‿ — | ‿

*12. still retains the name of Burnham.   — ‿ | — ‿ | — ‿ | — ‿

13. which being an early station   — | — ‿ ‿ | — ‿ | — ‿

14. it is not improbable   ‿ ‿ — | ‿ — | ‿ ‿

*15. the neighbour parts were filled with habitations,   ‿ — | ‿ — | ‿ — | ‿ — | ‿ — | ‿

*16. either of Romans themselves,   — ‿ ‿ | — ‿ ‿ | —

*17. or Britons Romanized,   ‿ — | ‿ — | ‿ —

*18. which observed the Roman customs.   ‿ ‿ — | ‿ — | ‿ — | ‿

[* An alternative scansion, somewhat more musical, of some of these clauses may be offered:

2.   ‿ ‿ — ‿ | — ‿ ‿ — | — ‿ ‿ —

3.   ‿ | — ‿ — | — — ‿

4.   — — | ‿ ‿ — ‿ | — ‿ <

6.   — — | ‿ — ‿ | — —

8.   ‿ — | ‿ ‿ — ‿ | —

10.   ‿ | — ‿ ‿ | — ‿ ‿ | —

12.   — ‿ — | ‿ — | ‿ — | ‿

15.   ‿ | — ‿ — | ‿ — | ‿ — | ‿ — | ‿

16. — ⏑ ⏑ | — ⏑ | ⏑ —

17. ⏑ — ⏑ | — ⏑ —

18. ⏑ ⏑ — | ⏑ — ⏑ | — ⏑

This, with the 5-time foot and the 6-time foot noted in the text, would give ten 5-time feet and three 6-time feet, i.e. thirteen feet of 5 or 6 times. Even so, however, such feet form less than 25 per cent. of the whole.]

In this passage, disregarding the odd syllables at the end of the clauses, there are about 59 feet.   37 of these, I think, are clearly iambuses (feet of 3 times), and 9 are anapaests (feet of 4 times).   There are 4 trochees, and 2 dactyls.   There is only one foot of 5 *times*, or at the most two; and only one foot of 6 *times*.   One or two of the feet are doubtful.   Of course you may not agree entirely with my scansion; that is too much to expect, in prose rhythms especially.   But the general result I think you will concede, viz. that out of the 59 feet, *about* 56 are short feet of 3 *times*, and only 2 or 3 are feet of 5 or 6 *times* (Paeonic or Ionic).   The disagreeable jog-trot effect is given by the 49 feet of anapaestic or iambic character.

Let us next look at a paragraph I have quoted already— the paragraph in which the *Jewish nation* should have been expressed as the subject.   Though it lacks construction, it is far better than his worst note-book style, and some of the individual clauses are excellent.   It is again from the *Urn-Burial* (p. 134, Dent's edition).

1. Nor in their long cohabitation   — | ⏑ — — / ⏑ ⏑ — | — ⏑ ⏑ ⏑ | — ⏑

2. with Egyptians,   ⏑ ⏑ — —

3. crept into a custom   — | ⏑ ⏑ ⏑ ⏑ — ⏑

4. of their exact embalming,   ⏑ — | ⏑ — | ⏑ — ‹

5. wherein deeply slashing the muscles,   — — | — ⏑ — | ⏑ ⏑ — ⏑ ⎫
    — — | — ⏑ — ⏑ | ⏑ — ‹ ⎭

6. and taking out the brains and entrails,   ⏑ — | ⏑ — | ⏑ — | ⏑ — —

7. they had broken the subject   ⏑ ⏑ — ⏑ | ⏑ — —

8. of so entire a resurrection,   ⏑ — | ⏑ — | ⏑ — | ⏑ — | ⏑

9. nor fully answered the types   — — ⏑ | — ⏑ ⏑ | —

10. of Enoch, Elijah, or Jonah,   ‿ — — | ‿ — — | ‿ — —

11. which yet to prevent or restore   — — | ‿ ‿ — | ‿ ‿ —

12. was of equal facility   ‿ ‿ — ‿ | ‿ — ‿ ‿

13. unto that rising power,   { — ‿ — | — ‿ — / ‿ ‿ — | — ‿ — / ‿ ‿ | — — ‿ — }

14. able to break the fasciations   — ‿ ‿ — | ‿ — — ‿ — ‿

15. and bands of death,   { ‿ — | ‿ — / ‿ | — ‿ — }

16. to get clear out of the cere-cloth,   ‿ — — | — ‿ ‿ | — —

17. and an hundred pounds of ointment   ‿ ‿ | — ‿ — | ‿ — <

18. and out of the sepulchre   ‿ — | ‿ ‿ — ‿ ‿

19. before the stone was rolled from it.   ‿ — | ‿ — | ‿ — | ‿ ‿ } / ‿ | — ‿ — | ‿ — ‿ ‿ }

These results are interesting. You notice first that iambuses and feet of an anapaestic character (i.e. feet of 3 *times* or 4 *times*) are not nearly so obtrusive, and that longer and more musical feet (containing the equivalent of 5 or more quavers) have correspondingly increased. There are about 50 feet in the passage. Quite 14 or 15, I think, may be regarded as feet of 5 *times*, and 5 as feet of 6 *times* or 7 *times*. That is to say, two-fifths of the whole are feet of 5 or more *times*. In the previous passage, you will remember, there was only 1 foot of 5 *times* (or possibly 2), and only 1 (or 2) of 6 *times*. You will further notice that the character of this paragraph is somewhat more imaginative than that of the previous passage, which consists largely of narrative jottings.

The next piece I shall ask you to look at is from the *Religio Medici*. It is almost, if not quite, on Browne's highest level, though it is not quoted by Saintsbury (who of course cannot give everything). In it we get Browne's vision of the Last Day and of the final justice. The recurrent phrase "This is the day" may possibly remind you of the refrain in Beethoven's C Minor Symphony—a refrain which Beethoven described in the words "So Fate knocks at the door."

1. This is the day

2. that must make good

3. that great attribute of God,

4. His Justice;

5. that must reconcile

6. those unanswerable doubts

7. that torment

8. the wisest understandings;

9. and reduce

10. those seeming inequalities,

11. and respective distributions

12. in this world,

13. to an equality

14. and recompensive Justice

15. in the next.

16. This is that one day,

17. that shall include and comprehend

18. all that went before it,

19. wherein

20. as in the last scene,   { ⏑ ⏑ ⏑ — | —
                        ⏑ ⏑ — —

21. all the Actors must enter,   — | ⏑ — — | ⏑ — <

22. to compleat and make up   ⏑ — — | ⏑ — —

23. the Catastrophe of this great piece.   ⏑ | ⏑ — ⏑ ⏑ | ⏑ — — —

24. This is the day   ⏑ ⏑ ⏑ —

25. whose memory hath onely power   — — ⏑ ⏑ | ⏑ — ⏑ —

26. to make us honest   ⏑ — ⏑ | — <

27. in the dark,   — ⏑ — }
                ⏑ ⏑ —

28. and to be vertuous   — ⏑ — | — ⏑ <

29. without a witness.   ⏑ — | ⏑ — <

In this passage there are about 50 feet. 32 of them (i.e. 64 per cent.) may be regarded as feet of 5 *times*, and perhaps 6 as feet of 6 or 7 *times*. That is to say, these longer feet (perhaps 38 in all) now make up about 75 per cent. of the whole. In passing, the balance of clauses 10 and 13, 11 and 14, 12 and 15, is worthy of notice.

I should now like to take two still more famous passages—both from the *Urn-Burial*. This is the first:—

1. Circles and right lines   — ⏑ | ⏑ — —

2 limit and close   { — ⏑ | ⏑ —
                — ⏑ ⏑ —

3. all bodies   — — ⏑

4. and the mortal right lined circle   ⏑ ⏑ — ⏑ | — — — — ⏑

5. must conclude and shut up all.   { — ⏑ — | ⏑ — — —
                  ⏑ — —

6. There is no antidote   ⏑ — — | — ⏑ —

7. against the opium of time   ⏑ — | ⏑ — ⏑ ⏑ | ⏑ —

8. which temporally considereth all things: — | — ⏑ ⏑ ⏑ | ⏑ — ⏑ ⏑ | — ·

9. our fathers find their graves   — — ◡ | — — — —

10. in our short memories,   ◡ — — | — ◡ <

11. and sadly tell us   ◡ | — ◡ — | —

12. how we may be buried   — — | ◡̆ ◡̆ = = | ◡̆   }

13. in our survivors.   ◡ — | ◡ — —

14. Gravestones tell truth   — — — —

15. scarce forty years   — | — ◡ —

16. generations pass   ◡ ◡ — ◡ | —

17. while some trees stand,   { ◡̆ — — | = / ◡̆ | — — — }

18. and old families   ◡ — | — ◡ <

19. last not three oaks.   — — — —

20. To be read by bare inscriptions   { ◡ ◡ | — ◡ — | ◡ — < / ◡ — — | ◡ — ◡ — ◡ }

21. like many in Gruter,   — — ◡ | ◡ — <

22. to hope for eternity   { ◡ | — ◡ — | — ◡ < / ◡ — | ◡ — — | ◡ ◡ }

23. by enigmatical epithets   ◡ | ◡ ◡ ◡ ◡ ◡ | — ◡ —

24. or first letters of our names,   ◡ | — — ◡ | ◡ — —

25. to be studied by antiquaries   { ◡ | — — ◡ | ◡ — ◡ ◡ / ◡ ◡ — ◡ | ◡ — — ◡ }

26. who we were,   — — —

27. and have new names given us   ◡ | — — — | — ◡ <

28. like many of the mummies,   — — ◡ | ◡ ◡ — ◡

29. are cold consolations   ◡ — — | ◡ — <

30. unto the students   { ◡ ◡ | ◡ = = / ◡ ◡ — | = }

31. of perpetuity,   ◡ | — ◡ — | ◡ ◡

32. even by everlasting languages.   — ◡ — | ◡ ◡ — ◡ | — ◡ <

In this passage there are about 64 feet. Of these, I
should regard 39 (i.e. 61 per cent.) as feet of 5 *times*, and

quite 9 as feet of more than 5 *times*. These long feet, then (of 5 *times* or more) here number 48; that is 75 per cent. of the whole.

Lastly let me take the first few lines of Chapter V. If it is frequently quoted, yet you will perhaps forgive a short examination of it. The general recognition of its greatness makes it the more interesting as a test case.

1. Now since these dead bones   — — — | — — —

2. have already outlasted   ∪ ∪ — ∪ | — — ∪

3. the living ones of Methuselah,   ∪ | — ∪ — | ∪ ∪ — ∪ ∪

4. and in a yard under ground,   ∪ ∪ ∪ — | — ∪ —

5. and thin walls of clay,   ∪ — — | ∪ —

6. outworn all the strong   — — | — ∪ —

7. and specious buildings above it,   ∪ | — ∪ — | ∪ ∪ ∪ ∪

8. and quietly rested   ∪ — ∪ ∪ | — ∪

9. under the drums and tramplings of three conquests;   ∪ ∪ ∪ — | ∪ — — | ∪ — — —

10. what prince can promise $\left. \begin{array}{l} = = | = = ∪ \\ = = | ∪ = < \end{array} \right\}$

11. such diuturnity unto his relicks,   — — ∪ | — — ∪ ∪ | ∪ ∪ ∪ ∪

12. or might not gladly say,   ∪ — — | — ∪ —

13. "Sic ego componi versus in ossa velim."

14. Time,   —

15. which antiquates antiquities,   ∪ | — ∪ — | ∪ — ∪ ∪

16. and hath an art to make dust   ∪ ∪ ∪ — | ∪ — —

17. of all things,   ∪ — —

18. hath yet spared these minor monuments.   ∪ — — | — — ∪ | — ∪ —

We have here then, let us say, 35 feet, excluding of course the Latin line, which has nothing to do with English prose rhythm. Out of the 35, I should reckon 26 as feet of

5 *times*, and 3 as feet of more than 5 *times*.   If in line 11
you take "relicks" as a long and a short, instead of two
shorts, then there would be 25 feet of 5 *times* and 4 of
more than 5 *times*.   But I think it should be two shorts.
In any case, 83 per cent. may be regarded as feet of 5 *times*
or more, and probably 74 per cent. as feet actually of 5 *times*.

Now what strikes me as interesting in the foregoing
analyses is this: that as Browne's work becomes more
imaginative and his style more musical; as he utters more
of his inner mind and less of his external observations; so
we catch more clearly this rhythm of 5 times (paeons,
cretics, etc.).   Of course the rhythm, as it must be in prose,
is varied, and broken by other feet; were it not so we should
have not prose but verse.   But this 5-rhythm, as a lovely
background, is unmistakably there: there is, as Saintsbury
might have said, an "underhum" of it.   In detail you may
quite possibly, as I said, not quite agree with the scansions
I have offered.   I myself, in some respects, venture to differ
from Saintsbury's analysis.   Yet, as a broad result, I
think we shall all· recognise that this 5-*time* rhythm is, in
Sir Thomas Browne's nobler passages, delightfully apparent
—is perhaps dominant.   When we spoke, a little time ago,
of the *Cyrus Garden*, we noted Browne's conviction that a
great part, both of nature and art, is permeated by the
number five—by the quincunx.   It is not incongruous,
then, in some of his own immortal work, to fancy we catch
this Underhum of the Quincunx, like some faint music
of the spheres.

It is time however to leave these detailed considerations,
and to turn to a more general view of Browne's literary
position.   We have already, in trying to form an idea of
the man and his writings, touched upon his life, and run
over the titles of his works; on the contents of some of these,
and on their style, we have lingered for a time.   We have
seen, too, how one or two scholars have regarded him—
Johnson, Pater, Symonds, Saintsbury.   In order that our
parting view of Sir Thomas Browne may be set in a large
perspective, let me recall to your memory the impression
he made upon De Quincey, Charles Lamb, and Coleridge.

That Charles Lamb was one of Sir Thomas Browne's

"protestants" is well known. Canon Ainger in fact goes so far as to say, in the Introduction to his edition of the *Essays of Elia* (Macmillan, 1883), that Lamb "knew the writings of Browne so well that not only does he quote him more often than any other author, but whenever he has to confront the mysteries of life and death his mental attitude at once assimilates to Browne's, and his English begins to dilate and become sombre. The dominant influence on Lamb in his reflective mood is Browne. His love of paradox, and the colour of his style, derived from the use of Latinised words never thoroughly acclimatised, is also from the same source." This, from so close a student of Lamb as Canon Ainger, is noteworthy. Now among the *Essays of Elia*, that on *The Two Races of Men* has a double appropriateness to our purpose, since it indicates the feelings both of Lamb and of Coleridge towards Browne. Lamb is describing "*borrowers of books*—those mutilators of collections, spoilers of the symmetry of shelves, and creators of odd volumes"; and he instances Coleridge (Comberbatch, he calls him) as "matchless in his depredations." Dwelling on these depredations, he says presently:—

"The slight vacuum in the left-hand case—two shelves from the ceiling—scarcely distinguishable but by the quick eye of a loser—was whilom the commodious resting-place of Browne on Urn Burial. C. will hardly allege that he knows more about that treatise than I do, who introduced it to him, and was indeed the first (of the moderns) to discover its beauties—but so have I known a foolish lover to praise his mistress in the presence of a rival more qualified to carry her off than himself." Lamb concludes the essay in these words. "Reader, if haply thou art blessed with a moderate collection, be shy of showing it; or if thy heart overfloweth to lend them, lend thy books; but let it be to such a one as S. T. C.—he will return them (generally anticipating the time appointed) with usury; enriched with annotations, tripling their value." Lamb then gives instances, from his own library, of books thus treated by Coleridge; and among the authors named is Sir Thomas Browne. Actually, we know that at all events Lamb's copy of Browne's *Vulgar Errors* was in this way enriched by Coleridge.

The essay on "The Two Races of Men" was issued in 1820, in the *London Magazine*.[13] In the preceding year there had appeared in *Blackwood's Magazine* a letter signed by G. J., also concerning Coleridge's habit of writing notes on the blank leaves and margins of books. G. J. is stated by Dr. Haney, in his Bibliography of Coleridge, to be James Gillman. This is the letter:—

Mr. Editor,
    It is well known to those who are in habits of intercourse with Mr. Coleridge, that not the smallest, and, in the opinion of many, not the least valuable part of his manuscripts exists in the blank leaves and margins of books; whether his own or those of his friends, or even in those that have come in his way casually, seems to have been a matter altogether indifferent. The following is transcribed from the blank leaf of a copy of Sir Thomas Brown's works in folio, and is a fair specimen of these *Marginalia*; and much more nearly than any of his printed works, gives the style of Coleridge's conversation.

G. J.

Then comes the transcript, which is as follows:—

"Sir Thomas Brown," he says, "is among my first favourites. Rich in various knowledge; exuberant in conceptions and conceits; contemplative, imaginative; often truly great and magnificent in his style and diction, though, doubtless, too often big, stiff, and *hyperlatinistic*; thus I might, without admixture of falsehood, describe Sir T. Brown, and my description would have this fault only, that it would be equally, or almost equally, applicable to half a dozen other writers, from the beginning of the reign of Elizabeth to the end of the reign of Charles the Second. He is, indeed, all this; and what he has more than all this, and peculiar to himself, I seem to convey to my own mind in some measure, by saying, that he is a quiet and sublime *enthusiast*, with a strong tinge of *fantast*; the humourist constantly mingling with, and flashing across the philosopher, as the darting colours in shot silk play upon the main dye. In short, he has brains in his head, which is all the more interesting for a little twist in the brains. He sometimes reminds the reader of Montaigne; but from no other than the general circumstance of an egotism

[13] December, pp. 623–5.

M

common to both, which, in Montaigne, is too often a mere amusing gossip, a chit-chat story of whims and peculiarities that lead to nothing; but which, in Sir Thomas Brown, is always the result of a feeling heart, conjoined with a mind of active curiosity, the natural and becoming egotism of a man, who, loving other men as himself, gains the habit and privilege of talking about himself as familiarly as about other men. Fond of the curious, and a hunter of oddities and strangenesses, while he conceives himself with quaint and humorous gravity, a useful inquirer into physical truths and fundamental science, he loved to contemplate and discuss his own thoughts and feelings, because he found by comparison with other men's, that they, too, were curiosities; and so, with a perfectly graceful and interesting ease, he put *them*, too, into his museum and cabinet of rarities. In very truth, he was not mistaken, so completely does he see everything in a light of his own, reading nature neither by sun, moon, or candle light, but by the light of the fairy glory around his own head; that you might say, that nature had granted to *him* in perpetuity, a patent and monopoly for all his thoughts. Read his *Hydrostaphia* [*sic*] above all—and, in addition to the peculiarity, the exclusive Sir Thomas Browness; of all the fancies and modes of illustration, wonder at, and admire, his *entireness* in every subject which is before him. He is *totus in illo*, he follows it, he never wanders from it, and he has no occasion to wander; for whatever happens to be his subject, he metamorphoses all nature into it. In that Hydrostaphia, or treatise on some urns dug up in Norfolk —how earthy, how redolent of graves and sepulchres is every line! You have now dark mould; now a thigh-bone; now a skull; then a bit of mouldered coffin; a fragment of an old *tomb stone*, with moss in its *hic jacet*; a ghost; a winding sheet; or the echo of a funeral psalm wafted on a November wind: and the gayest thing you shall meet with, shall be a silver nail, or a gilt *anno domini*, from a perished coffin top!—The very same remark applies in the same force to the interesting, though far less interesting treatise on the Quincuncial Plantations of the Ancients, the same *entireness* of subject! Quincunxes in heaven above; quincunxes in

earth below; quincunxes in deity; quincunxes in the mind
of man; quincunxes in tones, in optic nerves, in roots of
trees, in leaves, in everything! In short, just turn to the
last leaf of this volume, and read aloud to yourself, the
seven last paragraphs of chapter 5, beginning with the
words '*more considerable.*' But it is time for me to be in
bed. In the words of Sir Thomas Brown (which will serve
as a fine specimen of his manner), 'but the quincunxes of
Heaven (*the hyades or five stars about the horizon, at midnight
at that time*) run low, and it is time we close the five ports
of knowledge; we are unwilling to spin out our waking
thoughts into the phantoms of sleep, which often continue
precogitations, making cables of cobwebs, and wildernesses
of handsome groves. To keep our eyes open longer, were
to *act* our antipodes! The huntsmen are up in Arabia;
and they have already passed their first sleep in Persia.'
Think you, that there ever was such a reason given before
for going to bed at midnight; to wit, that if we did not, we
should be *acting* the part of our antipodes! And then, 'THE
HUNTSMEN ARE UP IN ARABIA'—what life, what fancy!
Does the whimsical knight give us thus, the *essence* of gunpowder tea, and call it an *opiate?*''

In conclusion, let us turn to De Quincey. In the course
of his essay on *Rhetoric*,[14] he discusses some of Milton's
beauties and defects; and then proceeds as follows:—

"Milton, however, was not destined to gather the *spolia
opima* of English rhetoric: two contemporaries of his own,
and whose literary course pretty nearly coincided with his
own point of time, surmounted all competition, and in that
amphitheatre became the protagonistae. These were Jeremy
Taylor and Sir Thomas Browne; who, if not absolutely the
foremost in the accomplishments of art, were undoubtedly
the richest, the most dazzling, and, with reference to their
matter, the most captivating of all rhetoricians. In them
first, and perhaps (if we except occasional passages in the
German Jean Paul Richter) in them only, are the two
opposite forces of eloquent passion and rhetorical fancy
brought into an exquisite equilibrium, approaching, receding
—attracting, repelling—blending, separating—chasing and

[14] *De Quincey's Works*, Vol. X., pp. 43-5. (Black, 1862.)

chased, as in a fugue, and again lost in a delightful interfusion, so as to create a middle species of composition, more various and stimulating to the understanding than pure eloquence, more gratifying to the affections than naked rhetoric. Under this one circumstance of coincidence, in other respects their minds were of the most opposite temperament: Sir Thomas Browne, deep, tranquil, and majestic as Milton, silently premeditating and 'disclosing his golden couplets,' as under some genial instinct of incubation: Jeremy Taylor, restless, fervid, aspiring, scattering abroad a prodigality of life, not unfolding but creating, with the energy and the 'myriad-mindedness' of Shakespere. Where, but in Sir T. B., shall one hope to find music so Miltonic, an intonation of such solemn chords as are struck in the following opening bar of a passage in the *Urn-Burial*—'Now, since these bones have rested quietly in the grave, under the drums and tramplings of three conquests,' etc. What a melodious ascent as of a prelude to some impassioned requiem breathing from the pomps of earth, and from the sanctities of the grave! What a *fluctus decumanus* of rhetoric! Time expounded, not by generations or centuries, but by the vast periods of conquests and dynasties; by cycles of Pharaohs and Ptolemies, Antiochi and Arsacides! And these vast successions of time distinguished and figured by the uproars which revolve at their inaugurations; by the drums and tramplings rolling overhead upon the chambers of forgotten dead—the trepidations of time and mortality vexing at secular intervals, the everlasting sabbaths of the grave!"

[NOTE.—Since the above was in type an interesting appreciation of Browne has appeared in Mr. Lytton Strachey's new volume *Books and Characters*, pp. 32—44. In it Browne's style and his Latinism are discussed with sympathy and acumen.

Perhaps I may be allowed the pleasure of illustrating from Mr. Strachey two points referred to on pp. 141—2 above. (i) As to Browne's scientific knowledge, Mr. Strachey considers that "Browne was scientific just up to the point where the examination of detail ends, and its co-ordination begins. He knew little or nothing of general laws; but his interest in isolated phenomena was intense. And the more singular the phenomena, the more he was attracted. He was always ready to begin some strange inquiry." (ii) As to the aphorisms in *Christian Morals*, Mr. Strachey even thinks that that work "almost reads like an elaborate and magnificent parody of the Book of Proverbs"].

Index

1